Development
in a Divided Country

Ben Turok

with

Ha-Joon Chang & João Carlos Ferraz

First published by Jacana Media (Pty) Ltd in 2011

10 Orange Street
Sunnyside
Auckland Park 2092
South Africa
+2711 628 3200
www.jacana.co.za

ISBN 978-1-77009-966-1

Set in Minion 10.5/14pt
Printed and bound by Ultra Litho (Pty) Limited, Johannesburg
Job No. 001414

See a complete list of Jacana titles at www.jacana.co.za

Contents

Preface to the series

As we go to press, the ANC is preparing to mark the centenary of its existence. This is a remarkable achievement for any political movement, with few precedents anywhere in the world. Even more remarkable is the fact that it has been the ruling party in South Africa for 16 years and remains the most powerful political force in the country, despite many shortcomings. The ANC may not rule forever, but it has made a huge impact on South Africa in every dimension of its existence, hence its history and present-day work merit special recognition.

This series 'Understanding the ANC Today' is an attempt to map in broad outlines the party's history, the external influences that shaped its policies and actions, the depth of the policy challenges it faced in the decades prior to its victory over apartheid, and the problems it is now confronting as a ruling party.

The scope of the whole series is vast. But the contributors are among the top thinkers in the ANC and they have not shirked exploring all these issues to the full. Since their writing deals with the realities facing all the people of the country, and shaping the future, the books should be of interest to the general public and not just members of the ANC and its allies.

It is our hope that the books will become standard texts in university courses and used in schools to broaden the understanding of our youth of where they come from and where the ANC would like to lead them. It is also our hope that the presentation of these books to the movement as a whole will encourage reading and study so that our cadres will be better prepared for the enormous but exciting tasks ahead as we plan for the new South Africa.

These books are not written in the spirit of propaganda. They are analytical and historical. They deal frankly and without reservation about the diverse influences on the ANC of many ideologies and historical experiences across the globe for over a century. At the same time the organic development of the movement as an indigenous force is also given its proper recognition.

Ben Turok

Introduction

Sixteen years after coming to power, one of the most common refrains in the ANC is 'Political power is not enough; we need to tackle the economy'. In the same vein, ANC documents repeatedly complain that 'the structure of the economy has remained the same for a century'.

Curiously, the limitations of a political transition without economic transformation have long been recognised across independent Africa, and the ANC's Strategy and Tactics document of 2007 noted that this also holds for South Africa. One does not have to accept the Marxist notion of 'smashing' the inherited state system, to appreciate that accessing economic power is a very different matter from taking over the government. Particularly in the modern economic system of interlocking international corporations and financial flows, ensuring that the ruling party has a purchase on the economy is a major difficulty. Yet the problem has received little attention in the ANC and its allies.

The reality is that prior to the election of 1994 the ANC's preparations for economic transformation were inadequate. While the RDP was an excellent document, it did not address transformation in the full sense of political economy. GEAR was a holding operation and, in the view of many, actually stalled the economy. It certainly did not lay the basis for transformation.

Thus, as the ANC moves to mark sixteen years of government, more and more people are demanding an approach to economic policy that goes beyond stabilisation and structural adjustment on the IMF model. This has taken the form of a call for a developmental state which will allow much more active state intervention in the economy coupled with a developmental agenda that will create employment and empower communities.

Unfortunately, the theoretical underpinnings for such an approach have not kept pace with these promptings, which result more from a recognition that former policies have not delivered a better life for all than from intellectual work. Furthermore, there is serious opposition from business, international financial institutions and the vast apparatus generating public opinion. This opposition is actually hegemonic in public discourse and inhibits progressive policy-making in the ANC.

It was because of these deficiencies that the author presented a series of lectures to the ANC Parliamentary Caucus in 2009 on current topics in development economics. The essays which follow are the result, with a few additions.

Part One, 'The Challenge of Development', opens with a discussion of the dual economy, which is the most fundamental problem in the country, being the main outcome of the apartheid system. Clearly, unless the government solves the problems generated by this divide, no amount of growth in the formal, advanced sector of the economy will 'trickle down' to the subsistence rural areas. Nor is it possible to make credible 'ladders' for the rural poor to enter the formal economy.

Then follows a discussion of the mixed economy and a recognition that a developmental state is not a command economy state but that it does indeed include and depend on a substantial private sector. This reality was endorsed and amplified by two visiting experts from South Korea and Brazil, whose essays in this book nevertheless insist on a major developmental role for the state, including the provision of investment capital.

Part Two, 'South Africa's Political Economy', analyses the economy in this classical tradition and includes dimensions such as the relation of race and class, job creation and economic choices. Also included are sections on BEE and why such transactions tend to fail, and the role of black business in relation to the aspirations of the liberation movement and white capital.

Part Three, 'The Global Environment', places the South African economy in the context of the international hegemony of neoliberalism and globalisation. As the essays argue, far from the global system offering opportunities to this country, the international trading and the financial systems pose enormous threats to the hope of South Africa breaking out of its distorted economic legacy.

The role of the IMF and World Bank is also discussed and the impact of the standard structural adjustment programmes across Africa is analysed. Reference is also made to the somewhat hidden impact these institutions have had on ANC and government policies and programmes. Both the ANC and the government have been rather shy of making public their negotiations with these institutions even though many agreements have been signed, largely covering technical support.

Several other essays deal with relations between the member states of the SADC region and the need for a comprehensive development integration programme. Also covered are the highly contentious Economic Partnership Agreements with Europe, which are dividing the region and inhibiting regional integration.

These lectures became the basis for the high-level series of seminars, *The Controversy about Economic Growth*, which followed and which are published in Volume 6 of this series.

Definitions and Key Terms

Broad-based industrialisation: industrialisation that includes smaller enterprises.

Budget deficit: occurs when government spends more money than it takes in. The opposite of a budget deficit is a *budget surplus*.

Decent work: good jobs and decent conditions in which work happens.

Development economics: *economic growth* is generally distinguished from *development economics*. Growth is primarily the study of how countries can advance their economies. Development is the study of the economic aspects of the development process in low-income countries.

Developmental imperatives: includes infrastructure, markets, training, etc.

Developmental state: the state has more independent, or autonomous, political power, as well as more control over the economy. A developmental state is characterised by having strong state intervention, as well as extensive regulation and planning.

Economic growth: the increase in the amount of the goods and services produced by an economy over time. It is conventionally measured as the per cent rate of increase in real gross domestic product (GDP) and in inflation-adjusted terms, in order to adjust for the effect of inflation on the price of the goods and services produced.

Exchange rate: specifies how much one currency is worth in terms of another designated currency. It is the value of a foreign nation's currency in terms of the home nation's currency.

Fiscal policy: the use of government spending and revenue collection to influence the economy.

Frontiers of poverty: identifies the scale of poverty.

Income inequality: the proportion of income between the rich and the poor.

Interest rate: the price a borrower pays for the use of money they do not own; for instance, a small company might borrow from a bank to kick-start their business, and the return a lender receives is normally expressed as a percentage rate over the period of one year.

Macroeconomic model: explains the relationship between such factors as national income, output, consumption, unemployment, inflation, savings, investment, international trade and international finance.

Microeconomics model: primarily focused on the actions of individual agents, such as firms and consumers, and how their behaviour determines prices and quantities in specific markets.

Monetary policy: attempts to stabilise the economy by controlling interest rates and the supply of money.

State-led industrial policy: where the state enables, facilitates and opens up new areas for industrial development.

Sustainable and inclusive growth: economic growth that includes the many rather than the few.

Sustainable livelihoods: incomes that are ongoing, not casual.

Transformation of the economy: moving away from the inherited apartheid model.

Part One

The Challenge of Development

Chapter 1

The Dual Economy

In 1999, when I returned from 25 years in exile, I drove around Gauteng to see what had happened during my long absence. I noticed many more industrial buildings in Midrand, and high-rise buildings and new factories in the middle of Johannesburg, all surrounded by squatter camps. During my years of exile, attending conferences in around 120 countries, I visited many cities, especially in the Third World. Gauteng reminded me of Mexico City or many large cities in Africa and India. As you fly into Mexico City or Abidjan, for example, the big buildings you see suggest that you are arriving in a highly developed country. However, when you land and drive into town, you see squatter camps. Similarly, when you fly into Cape Town you first see beautiful scenery, and then you see the shacks of Khayelitsha. Based on the comparisons I drew between Johannesburg and Mexico City, Abidjan and New Delhi, I wrote a short paper entitled 'The Skyscraper Economy', in which I described South Africa as this dual economy – a mixture of extreme wealth and power and extreme poverty. I began to develop this idea of the skyscraper economy as typical of the Third World. You can see the same phenomenon throughout the Third World – in New Delhi, Bombay, Kuala Lumpur. As you fly in, you see the impressive tall buildings, and then you land and see *spaza* shops, hawkers in the street and masses of very poor people.

Why dualism?

To answer the question of why we have this dualism between the rich centre and the poor periphery, we turn to the work of André Gunder Frank, a German economic historian and sociologist who spent many years in Brazil. In a seminal paper (later a book) called 'The Development of Underdevelopment', Gunder Frank wrote that underdevelopment means that a society or country has been developed downward. It does not mean that a country is undeveloped (for example, that there is no transport infrastructure). The development of underdevelopment is a process. Gunder Frank said that capitalism has penetrated the Third World through colonialism and imperialism. By penetrating economies like Brazil, it has created a modern sector in the cities, but this development has simultaneously underdeveloped the rural areas. Capitalism develops factories, buildings and infrastructure in cities, but the rural areas pay for this development. So the exploitation of the rural areas enriches the cities.

The origins of dualism in South Africa

When the British arrived in Natal, they found that there were a lot of Africans in the villages and rural areas, and they wanted them to come and work on their farms. The way they did this was to levy a hut tax. But the people resisted, opposing the tax. If you live in a village and have to pay a tax on your hut, you have to find money somewhere. People were living in a subsistence economy, not a cash economy. The tax forced people out of their villages onto white farms, and marked the beginning of dualism. In effect, it was the beginning of apartheid.

Subsequently, when the mining industry needed labour they used all kinds of mechanisms to force people to work on the mines. The Chamber of Mines used the system of the Witwatersrand Native Labour Association (WNLA, or Wenela) to get labour from all over southern Africa. They sent lorries, buses and aircraft to fetch people, and established depots in various countries to process workers. It was the beginning of the migrant labour system. When you remove labour from a rural area, you underdevelop that area, because the fittest and strongest young people are withdrawn to go and work in the first economy. This creates underdevelopment.

Underdevelopment occurred throughout the Third World. In Brazil, for example, there were *latifundia*, a Spanish word for large agricultural estates. The owners of these big farms needed the labour of the peasants, so they introduced all sorts of measures to force them out of the peasant economy. This resulted in the development of underdevelopment; dualism arises from this process. Effectively, the development of underdevelopment means that one area becomes developed while another area remains underdeveloped.

Many scholars have adopted and developed Gunder Frank's idea. In South Africa, dualism developed to the extent that today the former homelands have become a kind of reservoir where you find little real economic activity and much dependency on social welfare grants. You also find a lot of slackness in work, and the economy is not flourishing. Why is this happening? When I was attending an *imbizo* near East London, I drove around the whole area and thought it felt like a suburb of Johannesburg or East London. These homeland areas have become suburbs; people live there and they go to work in a town and return to see their families. But these areas are not economically viable entities because they depend on grants and handouts. This situation is typical of the Third World. But in a country like India, with a similar system, the peasants are building their own rural economy, and this is one of the reasons the Indian economy is growing so fast. In South Africa, apartheid smashed the rural economy because of the need for labour and to exert political control.

The question of dualism is a critical one for South Africa.

Unfortunately the African National Congress (ANC) has not grappled with it effectively. I was much struck by this at a seminar with Minister Jabu Moleketi, in Midrand, around the time of the Polokwane conference in 2007. The Minister said that he had been to the Eastern Cape for a meeting with comrades; they had tackled him on the question of dualism and he had to confess that the ANC had until then lacked an economic policy for rural development. However, Polokwane produced an excellent policy document on rural development, marking the beginning of an acknowledgement and understanding that we have a dual economy. Johannesburg and Cape Town can keep growing, but the rural areas will remain underdeveloped because apartheid sucked the blood from them

What Gunder Frank did was to say that the reason Brazil had a dual economy was because capitalism penetrated the cities but also the rural areas, subjecting the whole country to capitalist exploitation. In South Africa the rural areas were subjected to capitalist exploitation by the mines and the farming industry. However, Joe Slovo once wrote that while it is true that capitalism has penetrated the rural areas in Brazil and in South Africa, capitalism in rural areas is different to capitalism in urban areas. This is an important idea, although Slovo's important contribution was somehow never adopted as ANC policy. Capitalism is not universal in the way it works; it is not just one system, but rather has various subsystems. When people in the rural areas are exploited, it is not the same as the exploitation of a mineworker in Johannesburg or a retail store worker in Cape Town. It is very important to understand this difference theoretically and analytically. How is a peasant in the Transkei exploited? How is a mineworker or factory worker in Johannesburg exploited? If you are going to discuss the economy, you need to understand these differences in order to find appropriate solutions. The solution for the rural areas is not the same as the solution for the cities.

In several speeches, former president Thabo Mbeki said there is a structural fault in the South African economy. In geology, a structural fault occurs when a weakness in the earth's crust causes a piece of the surface to be displaced. What Mbeki was saying is that the South African economy is not an even economy or the same throughout the country. The fault is signalled by the difference between the first economy and the second economy. Many economists, academics and theorists, especially those who are slightly socialist in orientation, are unhappy with the terms 'first economy' and 'second economy'. They argue that South Africa is one economy, not two economies, and when you use the word 'dual', you are acknowledging the existence of two economies. Many comrades argue that it is wrong even to talk about the first economy and the second economy.

The second economy is a metaphor; it is a substitute term for the peripheral parts of the South African economy. Gunder Frank talked about the centre and the periphery – the city is the centre and the periphery is the rural area. He defined the development of underdevelopment as the centre undeveloping the periphery. I use the term 'the periphery' as well to refer to the second economy, located mainly in urban townships and the rural areas. However, this premise is surprisingly controversial. When I did some research I found it was not easy to get accurate information. I asked Statistics South Africa (SSA) to tell me how many people live in the rural areas. They offered a figure of about 15 million people. However, I think this is an underestimate. Then I asked a more difficult question: how many people live in the townships in South Africa? They could not answer this question. They do not know how many people live in the townships. I arrived at a figure of 9 million living in the townships (a huge underestimation) and 15 million in the rural areas. Thus 24 million people, or half of South Africa's total population, live in what I call the second economy. This is what interested me, not the demographics. I am interested in the economic implications. You cannot design an economic policy if you do not know who lives where.

To illustrate my point, consider the story of a company that wanted to sell shoes in the Caribbean. They sent a commercial salesman to a Caribbean island to establish what size shoes people wore. He walked around, saw tall and short people and he came up with an average of size 7. The company then produced 10 000 pairs of shoes, which they sent to the island, but nobody bought the shoes. Our statistics work like that – they provide data that does not help us develop policy. If you do not know how many people live in the townships across the whole of South Africa, how can you make policy for the townships? Again, if we do not have accurate figures for the people living in former homelands, how do we make rural policy?

For years I have been saying that the second economy consists of people living in the rural areas and the townships. For the record, when you look at statistics of unemployment for rural and urban areas, the data are the same.

When you make policy, you need to step back and see what the essential contradiction is. The essential contradiction is that the exploitation of labour is the same in rural and urban areas, except that it takes place in a different way. The Polokwane Rural Development Resolution was important because it acknowledged that difference. In South Africa we must understand the essential structural fault. I want to expand on this a little. I have been in the Trade and Industry Committee for 15 years, and when Alec Erwin was Minister they kept telling us that the future of the South African economy lay in manufacturing exports. But what about the people in the townships and rural areas who are not working? Are these people going to be helped by manufacturing industry in Midrand exporting? We need to get to the heart of this problem, which is that manufacturing industry alone is not the solution to South African poverty, inequality and unemployment.

While the Polokwane Rural Development Resolution goes a long way, it is only a beginning. The work must be continued by people who come from the rural areas, not somebody based at Wits University. Our problem has been that even ANC policies are written by people in urban areas who understand the city better. I understand the modern economy fairly well, and frankly I don't understand the rural economy. When I went on holiday to Coffee Bay, I walked around the area and saw little growing and nothing happening, and I don't understand why. Is there no initiative or no energy? We need to be able to explain this situation.

The process of underdevelopment, created under apartheid, resulted in millions of people being unable to enter the formal economy, due to a lack of assets or opportunities, or to generate self-sustainable development. These people survive through informal trading, survivalist activities, family remittances and social grants. That is the reality.

I am an activist as well as an academic. My approach is, what do we do with our country? Are we doing the right thing? Our objective, as the ANC, should be to define solutions. When you are looking for solutions, you can find micro-solutions at the local level (for example, *spaza* shops, traders, hawkers, internal trade, markets), but first you must ask what the problem is and how to fix it. In my view, the biggest problem in South Africa is the continuation of apartheid in some forms. We have abolished many laws and yet we still have dualism, we have a skyscraper economy; we have huge poverty and one of the highest levels of inequality in the world.

In 1955 I drafted the economics clause of the Freedom Charter, and I presented that clause at the Congress of the People. Yet every day, after 15 years in Parliament, I ask myself: are we sharing the country's wealth? Nobody can tell me that we all share in the economic wealth. This is proved by the Gini coefficient, which measures inequality: income inequality in

South Africa is higher than it was in 1994, and the economy is not being shared. We have to ask ourselves: are we pursuing the right policies to share the economy?

Discussion
Unemployment and employment statistics offer some very interesting data, but how do you define who is unemployed? If you look at the definition of unemployed persons, this covers somebody who works one hour a week for cash. So if a casual worker, a car guard, cleans your car for an hour and you give him R5, he is statistically employed. That means, in a way, that there is no unemployment in South Africa, as very few people don't work for one hour a week. I have written to the director of Statistics South Africa and asked him to explain how he can use such a definition, which implies that unemployment is almost nonexistent. In every township in South Africa, there are people who sell a cigarette or a bar of soap for an hour a week and thus, according to the definition, are employed.

While we still have apartheid structures within the economy, nationalisation is not the only solution. In many countries, there are different mechanisms of regulation, of intervention in the economy, that fall short of nationalisation. There are many ways, and we will return to this issue later.

My view is this, and it may not be a general view; we have such huge unemployment and so many people are becoming dependent on small social grants. Let me give you an example. The road from Mthatha to Coffee Bay is littered with potholes, and tourist buses damage the road even further. Why can't we suggest to the surrounding villages that government provides a certain amount of money per month if they fix the road? It's not glorifying work, but why can't we ask communities what they need? I believe, and this may be wrong, that we need to take small steps to uplift people and encourage them to grow something.

Karl Marx talks about social formations and modes of production. Now the mode of production in the Transkei is different to that in Gauteng; it's a rural mode of production, and there is no way you can say it is the same as the city. You have to draw a distinction between two modes of production because the one is a peasant mode of production and the other a modern, industrial mode of production. The extraction of surplus value is different. The peasant in the Transkei has surplus value extracted from him indirectly, but the urban industrial worker has surplus value extracted in a different way. Conceptually and theoretically we must say that there is one economy but with sub-sectors, so that you can distinguish between the relative modes of exploitation and explore what remedies to use.

At a conference in Pretoria, I served in a commission with former deputy president Phumzile Mlambo-Ngcuka, and we discussed this question of dualism. Government came with ladders: they said we must create ladders for the people from the rural areas or from the second economy into the first economy. How many ladders are we going to need in Pondoland, or Ciskei, to move into Johannesburg? It's an unrealistic formula. Let's understand how the economy works in Pondoland, and see what remedies we can apply there based on the mode of production and exploitation. You cannot apply the same measures to Midrand. If you want to come up with solutions, you must analyse thoroughly and specifically.

If you read the literature from the Development Bank and others, they say what we are going to do in a very superficial way. They say that development corporations do not work and people become corrupt. Mike Muller, the former director general of Water Affairs and Forestry, wrote an article in *Business Day* about 10 years ago saying, forget about rural areas, let them all come to town. Nobody challenged him. I said to him: are you crazy? Do you want 15 million people to come to Cape Town? Look what has already happened here. You have to ask why the

ANC, which is so strong and depends on votes in the Transkei and other rural areas, has no theory around rural development.

The Reconstruction and Development Programme (RDP) spent a lot of time on this question, and government ignored it. We are so keen on foreign investment and being like America and having large industries. There was a time when President Mbeki referred to the RDP in every speech, saying 'this is our vision', and this does not happen anymore. We don't have a vibrant economic discussion within the ANC. What we do is we sit round a table; the Minister comes and is worried about the press. He's very respectable and responsible and says things like prudence, caution, we don't touch business, we will never nationalise.

This is the dialogue. While the ANC talks of transformation, government does not do it. In many documents we refer to people-centred, people-driven development, but you cannot tell me that rural people in Mpumalanga are driving development in the area. I live in Cape Town, and you cannot tell me that the farmworkers in Worcester are driving development in the Western Cape. I do not want to be too radical here. The ANC came to power in a negotiated settlement. We had the sunset clauses and all that, and we told the public service we would not nationalise. We made commitments about what we would and would not do, within the old framework, which was not a transformative framework. But I am going to be radical here. When I was writing my book *From the Freedom Charter to Polokwane: The Evolution of ANC Economic Policy*, I wasn't happy with the title of the last chapter, which is usually where you summarise what has been said in the book. I chose to call the chapter 'Stalled in Orthodoxy', which I think is absolutely right. I believe, and this is where I am going to be attacked, that the ANC and the government have gotten into a mindset of stagnant orthodoxy. Polokwane was a kind of revolution and opened the door to new thinking, like Pravin Gordhan's statement about stimulus in the 2009 Treasury Budget Vote. A year earlier you would not have heard such a statement. I think we have got stuck in old formulae, in policy terms, in orthodoxy. We need to change that.

Why are we stuck? Looking back to the battles of 1995, the document outlining the RDP was brilliant. I gave a copy to former Tanzanian president Julius Nyerere during his visit to Johannesburg, and he called me to say that Africa had never seen such a document since independence. Yet within a year we had moved into the Growth Employment and Redistribution (GEAR) strategy. In my view, that shift set us back a long way.

I want to highlight one paragraph in Finance Minister Pravin Gordhan's 2009 speech introducing the Treasury Budget Vote, which is critical to everything we say and do. Gordhan says that reducing spending now will add to the weakness of the economy, and this will have a great impact on the poor and the vulnerable. We do not want to reduce the budget and spending, and so we are going to borrow and, of course, pay interest. The Minister says that we must maintain the strong growth of spending. This is countercyclical economics: when the economy is going down and the banks don't want to lend and there is a tightening of the whole financial sector, strong state spending is required to avert economic collapse. This is what Barack Obama is doing, what the Germans are doing and what the whole world is doing. It's called a stimulus. As the economy slides down, instead of saying our revenue is down, our taxes are down, so we must spend less, Gordhan says we must spend more because we want to release money into the system and create demand. This represents a major shift in the way we discuss economic policy and finance policy. It is the first time under ANC rule that our country has said that, and it took a lot of fighting to achieve. I was at the Alliance Economic Summit, just before the 2009 general election, and I can tell you that the Congress of South African Trade Unions (COSATU) fought hard for this sentence.

This highlights the need to educate ourselves on key issues. The key issue is: what is driving our perspective in this economy? Is it reduced spending? Is it caution? Is it budget surplus, or keeping the economy alive, and in what way? This is the critical issue.

Sources

Mbeki, Thabo (2003). 'Towards a people-centred new world order'. Speech, October 2003.

Webster, Eddie (2004). 'The dual economy', in *New Agenda: South African Journal of Social and Economic Policy*, Issue 15, Third Quarter, 2004.

Frank, André Gunder (1966). *The development of underdevelopment.* New York: Monthly Review Press.

Turok, Ben (2008). *From the Freedom Charter to Polokwane: the evolution of ANC economic policy.* Cape Town: New Agenda.

Chapter 2
The Mixed Economy

The role of the media

I am constantly concerned at how the press misleads us, and will begin by citing several examples. On 3 July 2009, *Business Day* ran a front-page story about the Minister of Finance headed 'Policy prudence bolstered South Africa's credit ratings'. The article suggested that the main thrust of the Minister's speech was prudence or caution, but buried in the report you find that Pravin Gordhan actually said that South Africa can afford to maintain present spending levels and increase borrowing to offset the revenue loss. This is not prudence. What the Minister said was that tax revenue in the last quarter had fallen by R20 billion, and over a whole year this could reach R60 billion – a major loss in taxation due to the fact that the economy has slowed down and so companies are paying less tax. The media immediately speak of 'prudence', but in fact the Minister said that we *can* afford to continue spending and we will borrow if we have to because reducing our spending level would further weaken the economy and impact on the poor and the vulnerable.

This is a central issue for the ANC in regard to where we are currently and where we are going. We want to reduce wasteful spending, and Minister Gordhan plans to do that, but overall we must not reduce our spending because that will weaken the economy and that will further burden the poor. In South Africa, we need to adopt and follow countercyclical policies, as confirmed by Minister Gordhan in his speech. While reducing waste is a good thing, governments should not reduce the amount of money in the economy, but rather borrow if necessary to maintain economic activity. This can lead to inflation and other consequences, but you have to make a decision to keep the economy moving by maintaining sufficient liquidity, borrowing if necessary and maybe even increasing taxation, because the alternative is sinking deeper and deeper into recession. This example highlights how the media provides wrong information about ANC policy; it is important for people to be aware of this bias.

There is a huge debate raging internationally on this issue, reflected for months in the pages of the London *Financial Times*. I recently met someone from KPMG headquarters in Germany who confirmed that wherever there is a recession – in the UK, Germany, France or the US – governments say we must not reduce our spending, and in fact we must maintain spending or risk weakening the economy as it falls deeper and deeper into recession. In 1929, governments did not keep money in the system, and that's why the recession became a depression; it took five years before the economy in the US began to revive. Today, because of the lessons of the past, governments are pumping money into the economy to keep it turning over and prevent a deeper depression or recession.

Economic profile of the economy

In thinking about the mixed economy, I spoke to two top economists. When I asked them for a profile of the South African economy, they were unable to provide one. About twenty years ago, Dr Z Rastomjee wrote a book entitled *The Political Economy of South Africa*, which gave a good picture of the apartheid economy. The book contained tables showing the size of the private sector and state-owned enterprises. Today, there is nothing like that. We do not have a picture of the South African economy. If you ask me how big the economy is, I can't answer except with bits and pieces of information, which is not satisfactory if we are to assist development in this country.

If we say South Africa is a mixed economy, which are the strong parts and which are the weak parts? I asked these questions in Parliament of Alec Erwin, the former Minister of Public Enterprises, about the number of public enterprises and their employees, turnover, total assets, annual profit and the role they play in the economy. When my questions were not answered, I went to him personally and asked why. He replied that his officials were still looking for the answers and he didn't have them. After making a nuisance of myself, he gave me a piece of paper showing the number of state-owned enterprises and their scale. According to this, in 2006/07 Eskom had 32 000 employees, annual turnover of R40 million, total assets of R143 million and profit of R6 million; Denel had 7 000 employees, R3 million turnover, R4 million assets and a loss of R500 000; Transnet had 48 000 employees, a total turnover of R28 million, total assets of R77 million and an annual profit of R6 million. This gives an indication of the size and scale of the state sector in the economy.

According to *Business Day*, small, medium and micro enterprises (SMMEs) contribute 35 per cent to GDP, employ 3.8 million people (34 per cent of formal employment and a third of the population in the formal sector). In the mining sector, the total expenditure of the Chamber of Mines in 2008 was R40 billion (R400 000 million) and dividends were R24 billion (*Business Day*, 25 August 2009). While these figures give some sense of the size of this sector, according to the Chamber of Mines the mines' assets are only a small portion of the wealth they create because of knock-on effects and downstream activities, which account for 7 per cent. So, for example, while the Chamber of Mines employs 500 000 people, an additional 500 000 people are employed to service that sector. So, if you nationalise the Chamber of Mines, you are nationalising 500 000 workers, but by their activity they feed another 500 000 people.

It's important to remember that where there is a factory, the people who work there are feeding the people outside who are selling Coca-Cola or food. If you close that factory, you close down those people too. There is a 'downstream' effect, and this is what happens with regard to unemployment. You can never isolate an industry; there is always a sector that supports this industry.

South Africa is a dual economy. We do have an advanced-technology sector, which requires skills. Our banks are considered among the best in the world. We have the best deep mining engineers in the world, and we sell that skill to other countries, even Russia. On the other hand, we also have a huge undeveloped section of the economy. If we are going to meet the requirements of our people and fulfil our economic programme and vision, we need massive training. Under the National Party, the apprenticeship system was widespread – all agencies and the railways had apprenticeship systems. I would put a further educational training college in every town in South Africa. If we spent more of our budget on that, I think we would be moving in the right direction.

For further data on the profile of the economy, I looked at statistics in the most recent quarterly bulletin (for 2009) of the South African Reserve Bank. I looked at a table on fixed capital formation (capital that is created in a particular sector), and what I found interesting is the relative scale of state, private sector and public-owned enterprises. Central government created fixed capital of R600 billion in 2008; the public corporations created R465 billion; but the private sector created about R1.4 trillion. In terms of a relative ratio, if the private sector made R1.4 trillion, the central government created a third of that and the public corporations created even less. That is why we talk about a mixed economy in South Africa.

In trying to understand the South African economy, there is no question that the private sector is the dominant and most powerful sector. If you look at the Johannesburg Stock Exchange (JSE), 70 per cent of the investment in shares is foreign. So South Africa is not even owned by South Africans. This is why the Department of Finance and the National Treasury are often very cautious in what they say, because if they say something radical or revolutionary foreigners may pull out of the stock exchange. Foreigners can go and invest in Hong Kong, Singapore, New York, and so on. There is no control over foreign capital, so foreign investors can move out anytime. If you look at capital in South Africa, the state-owned sector (e.g. Transnet, Eskom, SAA) is far smaller than the private sector. It is important to understand what a mixed economy means in South Africa.

China is a mixed economy, even though it is run by a communist party. The difference is that the Chinese government owns the banks. When I was in China and met chief economists there, I asked why they do not have private banks. They answered that the banking sector is the ultimate controlling force in the country. Even though you and I can do business in China, the economy, financial sector and finances of the country are controlled by the government (namely, the Communist Party of China).

Each mixed economy is different, as each country has a different profile. I wish that some of our top economists would give us a really clear picture of the economy in South Africa, as the picture we have is twenty years old and quite out of date. In my book, *From the Freedom Charter to Polokwane: The Evolution of ANC Economic Policy*, I presented some statistics to give a picture of the South African economy: 5 per cent of South Africans earned 88 per cent of the country's wealth; 10 per cent of the population (namely, white people) owned 87 per cent of the land; Africans owned 13 per cent of the land. Ownership of wealth and share capital was highly concentrated; in 1993, four large corporations (Anglo American, Rembrandt, SA Mutual/ Old Mutual and Sanlam) controlled 81 per cent of the share capital. Has this changed since 1993? Until we understand the role and size of each sector of our economy, there is not much we can do. We need scientific information. Sadly, it has been a long time since we actually did this critical analysis.

The market economy

Let us turn to some definition of issues. What is a market economy? What is the market? If you go to any township, there is a market there with people buying and selling. But it is not only goods that people buy; there is also a capital market. What does the capital market mean? Simply put, it is a place where you borrow money. Bankers, directors general and ministers of finance run around the world looking for capital to borrow. They too are faced with interest rates and an international market where people negotiate capital in different forms. One of these forms is the stock exchange.

What is the stock exchange? The stock exchange is a place where companies are listed, together with prices for their shares. The shares are then traded internationally. An American can come to the JSE and buy shares in a British company, or a Frenchman can use the Internet to trade American shares on the JSE. The JSE is a market where people buy and sell shares. When people buy and sell, the prices of shares go up and down. The stock exchange changes by the minute, with transactions amounting to billions of rands daily. Traders are buying and selling all the time. Their job is to make a profit; they have to make an assessment and say, for example, the shares in South Africa are going up because there is a good Minister of Finance and Reserve Bank, and so we will buy there. When the price goes up, they sell.

Our currency is tradeable. We used to have a regulated exchange rate, related to the dollar and the pound, but we freed that up. So the rand fluctuates, depending on the market. In 1992, financier George Soros made a huge profit by speculating against the value of the British pound. Currency speculators buy a lot of rands. When they buy, the value of the rand rises, and then they sell quickly and make a profit because the rand is high. Once they sell, the rand falls and is low. That's what is meant when the rand is described as 'stronger today': it means that the exchange rate is down. If you are going overseas and want to buy pounds, a strong rand means you need fewer rands to buy one pound (say R10). When the rand is weak, you might need R15 to buy one pound. It is the ratio that is important. When the rand is strong, we import a lot and our exports are weak. This is good for the businessman who travels or who imports goods. As the ANC, we do not want a strong rand because this is bad for exporters. We have to consider the economy as a whole and ask: what is good for this economy? We want to create jobs here in South Africa. The ANC's economic policy is to increase economic production, which is favoured by a weaker exchange rate rather than a stronger one.

China has a strong currency, and they are keeping it strong. The US says that China must strengthen its currency in order to import American goods because its cheap currency makes it better to export. In general, people gamble with currency, and governments intervene. China has a very strong and stubborn policy, and they will not change the exchange rate of the *renminbi* (RMB) relative to the dollar. The Americans are fighting this, and say that the Chinese keep their currency at the same level all the time, which is to their advantage. The Chinese say that their domestic economy and exports are too important and they are not going to change their exchange rate.

There are ways of handling the exchange rate. The Reserve Bank can change the exchange rate using certain mechanisms. In a mixed economy there is a market for shares (the stock exchange) and markets for commodities. South Africa exports a lot of primary commodities, such as gold, diamonds and fruit. The world market fluctuates. The prices of gold and oil change hourly. The markets for these and other commodities are like international gambling. When I was at the University of Zambia in 1979, the price of copper was very high. Within two years it had fallen by a third and the Zambian government, which depended on this revenue, was in big trouble.

Similarly, when I arrived in Tanzania in 1966, President Nyerere had nationalised the sisal industry, which had been badly run before independence. It was the main and largest industry in Tanzania. Sisal was very popular because it could be used to make many things – shoes, sandals, rope, bags and mats. But within two years the price had collapsed, presenting the country with a major problem. Even today the price of sisal remains very low. So the main industry in Tanzania made a loss because the price of sisal fluctuated on the world market. The same applies to oil, the price (per barrel) of which has fluctuated dramatically over the past decades.

There is another market – the labour market. We have a labour market nationally, and there is an international labour market. There are people who work in one country and go to another and earn more there and then they go to a third country and earn more there too. In other words, they are selling their labour on the international labour market. Workers are paid a certain rate, but that rate fluctuates, particularly where there are no unions. Unions stabilise the labour market and give the working class a certain stability in their life.

When we talk about the market economy, we are also faced with monopolies. We still have a high degree of monopolisation. The Competition Commission in the DTI looks at monopolies and oligopolies and the ways these control markets and prices in South Africa. In one instance, the major banks were allegedly in collusion to fix interest rates. The Trade and Industry Committee called hearings in Pretoria and we summoned the big five banks. The banks got very nervous, and the bank presidents arrived with teams of lawyers and accountants. We told them that there was evidence of collusion around interest rates. The Reserve Bank sets the repo rate, which is the price of money sold by the Reserve Bank to commercial banks. Once the Reserve Bank changes the repo rate, the commercial banks react immediately. We told them that there was evidence that the banks had held a meeting at which they decided the interest rate would go up by 1 per cent. The banks claimed that there was no collusion or an agreement, but they acknowledged that they had met. We asked them why all the banks raised the interest rate by the same amount at the same time. They replied that that is competition.

The command economy

Let us turn to the command economy, which is another term for the Soviet economic system. What Lenin did after the Russian Revolution was to nationalise all industries, and the state took over ownership of the means of production. When Fidel Castro came to power in Cuba, the state took over all the American enterprises, nationalised them with no compensation and created a command economy. Before the revolution, Russia was a very backward country without a stable steel industry. The Communist Party in Russia put in place a huge electrification programme for the whole Soviet Union, and they built a powerful steel industry. Within a matter of ten or fifteen years, the Soviet Union became the second-largest steel producer in the world.

The lesson is that the state can pump the economy at a fast rate because it is highly concentrated and very effective. In South Korea, following the Korean War, the state assumed a strong role in directing the economy. After the Second World War, Japan set up a powerful planning institute, the Ministry for International Trade and Industry (MITI), which in fact organised the economy. Some years ago I visited Taiwan and met with the head of that country's Planning Commission, who told me he had 300 employees. He provided me with a book showing data about every aspect of the economy. That data is used to plan the economy. The head of the Planning Commission was the most senior minister in the Cabinet; that is how serious capitalist Taiwan was about planning.

When the state decides to act, it can be very energetic, influential and powerful. However, in the Soviet Union problems arose around the planning, monitoring and measurement of production in state enterprises. For example, take the production of locks: if the criterion used to monitor performance and measure production was the quantity of steel used, factory managers made very big locks, using large quantities of steel, but those locks were not very useful. Then the planners came along and claimed that this was cheating, and that the factory would be judged by how many locks were made. So the factory manager made small locks in large quantities. Under a command economy, where the state undertakes central planning, it is difficult to monitor what a factory manager is doing because they fiddle the system, even if this is not motivated by profit.

In Zambia, I once interviewed the manager of a soap factory, who said that they used to make cheap soap for the masses but that there was no profit involved. At the end of the year, the Minister of Finance would call him in and ask how much profit had been made that year. When he explained that the factory ran at a loss because of the price of the soap, the Minister gave permission for the factory to manufacture a certain proportion of luxury soap. The factory then began to make luxury soap, which was sold at a high price and realised large profits. But in time the factory manager became greedy, because his salary depended on his profit, and so he increased the amount of luxury soap produced and reduced the quantity of cheap soap. Gradually the factory shifted to producing luxury soap. This illustrates the difficulty of state control of an enterprise because of the introduction of the idea of profits. We have the same problem with our parastatals. The Treasury and the Minister of Finance have told Sasol, Eskom, SAA and other state-owned enterprises that they must make a profit. The only way for a state-owned enterprise to make a profit is to raise prices. When this happens, you are no longer serving the economy, but rather serving the bottom line.

In a command economy, giving direction to factories is a large problem, but not the only problem. In the Soviet Union, when a dress factory manager was told to increase the number of dresses produced at a cheaper price, the factory began producing one dress – of the same colour and size – for the whole population. So every shop in Moscow stocked exactly the same dress in large quantities, and of course people did not buy the dress. Another problem with the command economy is consumer choice; one of the things about capitalism is that competition means consumers have a wide choice. The private sector is good at offering consumer choice.

A central command economy can do a great deal, as the Afrikaners and the National Party knew. They created these companies because they understood clearly that you need state-owned enterprises to push the economy. The command economy can do certain things effectively, but once you reach a certain point, malfunctions arise in the economy and consumers get very unhappy. In Stalin's last years, consumers in the Soviet Union were very unhappy; the shops had few goods, and what they did stock was all the same because it was manufactured on a conveyer belt. The limit of a command economy still depends on what the market does and what the market absorbs; the market is an important instrument in the economy, which the command economy does not recognise or take account of. The market allows competition, it allows for people to use their energy. If everything is controlled from the centre, you cut that out. The command economy, or planning, must enable the economy to grow, but the economy must grow well with variety, consumer choice and so on. That is the dilemma of economics.

Nationalisation

Nationalisation has become a key issue, with many people saying South Africa must nationalise. When I wrote the economic clause of the Freedom Charter, it did not use the word 'nationalisation'. The clause says, firstly, that the people shall share in the country's wealth, and secondly, that the national wealth of our country shall be restored to the people. The mineral wealth beneath the soil, the banks and the monopoly industries shall be transferred to the ownership of the people as a whole. All other industry shall be controlled, and trade will be opened to all. This is not a controversial viewpoint. We did not use the word 'nationalisation' because it was always identified with the Communist Party and the command economy. The Freedom Charter was adopted in 1955, and many of us had in mind what happened after the Second World War, when many countries nationalised. In England, the Labour Party government nationalised certain industries, but did so in a different way to Cuba and Russia. Even today, if you read the financial press, people say that the British government has nationalised the banks. In the case of the Royal Bank of Scotland, the British government has taken over the majority shareholding. Even in the US, following the collapse of Lehman Brothers, the government bought majority shares in many banks. When Cuba and the Soviet Union nationalised, the state assumed complete control, appointed a public servant as manager, sacked all the shareholders and created state institutions.

In 1955, we wanted to ensure that the economy, which was owned by the minority whites, was transferred to the people as a whole, but we did not want to use 'communist' language. When we said that the mineral wealth of the country belongs to the people, and therefore must be transferred to the people, there was not a word about the state taking over. This was because the global climate was in favour of state controls and state regulation. People asked if we really thought we could run the gold mines in South Africa. Our answer was that we would get assistance from the Soviet Union, which had a very strong mining industry with plenty of engineers and technicians – as Russia still has today. We admitted that the liberation movement did not have engineers to run the mines, or even managers. The ANC did not have any managers in those days.

If we look at the current situation, firstly we need to ask: are we in any position to take over the mining industry, to nationalise? Do we have trustworthy engineers within government? Can the ANC government run the mining industry without the present owners? You have to decide about that. Secondly, we would have to pay compensation, as Zambia had to do during the 1970s. When Zambian president Kenneth Kaunda nationalised Anglo American's copper mines, the company refused to leave without compensation, so Kaunda had to pay. He also accepted that he did not have engineers and management to run the mines, so he signed a management agreement with Anglo American. Although the state nationalised the copper mines, Anglo American retained the management. When you retain management, you retain control. What happened in Zambia was an exercise on paper. The Zambian government paid a lot of money to Anglo, and yet Anglo stayed on. They were running the place and making profits until the mines became a loss-making enterprise after the price of copper fell. The situation has improved slightly, but is still very uncertain.

While politically, as the ANC, in line with the Freedom Charter, we would like to take control of the economy and the mining sector, we need to consider the following questions carefully: could we manage it? Have we got the management? Would we be able to pay compensation? Our economy has a lot of foreign ownership – around 70 per cent of the stock exchange, including shares in the gold mines – and nationalisation would lead to a total withdrawal of this capital. The final question to consider is whether we would get away with this move politically.

I am concerned that after 15 years the ANC government has not developed a plan to do these things. We suddenly want to nationalise, but the foundations for this are serious and it's a very big part of the economy. Before jumping into this hot boiling oil, we need to make sure we have the resources. Do you know what the consequences would be? Have you made a plan? Have you built an engineering industry that can sustain whatever you want to do? If you jump too fast without laying a solid foundation of skills, institutions, and so on, you can make a very serious mistake.

The first important thing to recognise in this debate is that South Africa is a capitalist country. We have a mixed economy, but it is a capitalist economy. Capitalism is based on shares, on ownership, on the Reserve Bank, which is linked to commercial banks. If you remove the stock exchange and share capital as the mechanism of ownership, what are you left with? You are left with the state. Yes, there would still be diamonds and infrastructure, but the state would own it. That would not be capitalism. If we talk of such a fundamental shift in the economy, we need to be explicit about that and face the consequences. Under capitalism, money is the equivalent and measure of goods.

All the world's central banks, as well as the International Monetary Fund (IMF), have gold stocks. Gold is the last holder of value. When inflation fluctuates, gold has a certain stability. The IMF has vast quantities of gold stored in New York. All governments store gold; it is the store of value. If a lot of gold is put on the market, the price falls. This creates a problem for us, because the value of our gold, which is our revenue to pay for goods, will also fall. I am not saying that nationalisation is impossible, but rather arguing that we need to make a scientific case for it, not an emotional argument.

If we want to change policy, we need thorough analysis and sound data. We need to come up with facts about, for example, the mining industry and its contribution to the South African economy. The mining industry is the country's main foreign exchange earner. If we were to lose this source of foreign exchange, our economy would be in very serious trouble, and we would be unable to import the things we need.

Sources

Abedian, Iraj et al. (1997). *Promises, plans and priorities: South Africa's emerging fiscal structures.* Cape Town: IDASA.

African National Congress (2007). Strategy and Tactics document, as adopted by the 52nd National Conference, 2007.

Chang, Ha-Joon (2008). 'South Africa paralysed by caution', in *New Agenda: South African Journal of Social and Economic Policy*, Issue 31, 3rd Quarter: pp 6–11.

De Beer, Frik & Hennie Swanepoel (2002). *Introduction to development studies.* Cape Town: Oxford University Press Southern Africa.

Republic of South Africa (1994). White Paper on Reconstruction and Development. Available from www.info.gov.za/view/DownloadFileAction?id=70427; accessed 22 December 2010.

Turok, Ben (2008). *From the Freedom Charter to Polokwane: the evolution of ANC economic policy.* Cape Town: New Agenda.

Turok, Ben (1989). *Mixed economy in focus: Zambia.* London: Institute for African Alternatives.

Chapter 3
The Developmental State: Towards a New Paradigm

When the Government of National Unity was installed in 1994, the ANC had already adopted the Reconstruction and Development Programme (RDP) as its principal policy instrument. Business and the press were initially hostile to the programme, suspecting a hidden left agenda. However the Cabinet was persuaded to adopt a White Paper on the RDP, with minor amendments to the original plan, and the country swung behind it with unanticipated enthusiasm. Even the public service, steeped in apartheid ideology, adopted the RDP in a show of support for the new government. President Mandela appointed a Minister of State for the RDP and the provinces created RDP commissions. Business, especially in the construction industry, energetically sought building contracts, and there was a widespread expectation that the economy would take off.

Unfortunately, cautious counsel prevailed that the government's domestic debt was too high, and the RDP was displaced in 1996 by the Growth, Employment and Redistribution programme (GEAR). RDP offices were closed down, budget austerity became the watchword and the economy went into decline.

After more than fifteen years of caution, as the statistics of persistent inequality, poverty and unemployment become ever more embarrassing, the ANC and the state are turning once again to the idea of development, under the concept of a 'developmental state', as the way out of their difficulties. While the role of the state is under deep consideration in South Africa, we are not alone. The global economic crisis has brought it into focus around the world. In the developed countries particularly, failures in the financial sector are leading to reconsideration of the state's regulatory functions.

The focus in South Africa has been different, largely because the nature of our crisis is different and the possible solutions are not primarily in the financial sector, even if that area too needs serious attention. The 'developmental state' has become the centre of our attention, although many different meanings are attached to the term.

However, at the root of the debate is a serious concern about the poor performance of the economy as a whole. This chapter will argue that, since the central problem facing the country is that a large part of its economically active population is not engaged in productive work, the central challenge for a developmental state is to find a way to correct this.

Productive work is not only required for the purposes of providing income and restoring personal dignity: it is also the principal mechanism to counter crime, alienation and other social ills (Turok, 2008b). 'Productive work' may also be a better formula than the current one of 'decent work', which does not stipulate the kind of work envisaged nor its contribution to economic development.

Examples from the 'Asian Tigers'

After the Second World War, South Korea was a very backward country economically, although the education system was quite effective. One of the country's principal strategies was to promote small enterprise on the back of state procurement policies. State institutions and state-supported firms in South Korea were obliged to procure locally, preferably from small firms, thereby giving them a lift up the ladder. Even foreign corporations had to produce evidence that imported materials or components were not available locally (Chang, 2008). The state also intervened to support infant industries, to give direction to manufacturing and to curb imports of luxury items – all of which had a beneficial effect on the current account. These policies resulted in massive growth during the 1960s and 1970s.

A word of caution is appropriate here. Many of the fast-growing economies of East Asia relied on autocratic top-down rule, but this is not feasible in South Africa. We are committed to a democratic developmental state. No other model will fly here.

Japan, South Korea and Taiwan all successfully pursued the 'developmental state' route. Their governments pressured capital to move from rent-seeking behaviour[1] into investment in productive enterprises, mainly manufacturing. Land reform also gave the state a sound base among the peasantry. A key lesson is that the state's autonomy allowed it to discipline business. Private enterprises that sought contracts, export licences or any other facilities from state institutions had to comply with the overall industrial strategy of the state. The state also maintained control of the banks and the currency. In China, the ruling Communist Party still controls the main banks and appoints the managers of the main state enterprises. The state thereby maintains control over the key levers of the economy, even as it allows the private sector and foreign companies a great deal of leeway. Conversely, the state in South Africa has generally been unable or unwilling to direct and discipline business, and this has been a major factor stalling industrialisation and development. As a result, we have an economic system with low value-added in manufacturing and high propensity for rent-seeking.

South Africa also has much to learn from the so-called Asian

---

1 The expenditure of resources in order to obtain abnormal economic gain without reciprocating any benefits back to society through wealth creation. Examples would include individuals or groups lobbying for taxation, spending and regulatory policies that confer financial benefits or other special advantages upon them at the expense of taxpayers, consumers or others. (Dr Paul M. Johnson, Glossary of Political Economy Terms. Available from http://www.auburn.edu/~johnspm/gloss/rent-seeking_behavior; accessed 22 December 2010.)

Tigers about helping the backward areas of our economy to become productive. Indeed, it may be that raising productivity in underdeveloped areas, such as the former homelands, could do more to raise GDP than would concentrated efforts in already developed industries. It would certainly do more to alleviate poverty. This position was advanced in the rural development paper adopted at Polokwane in 2007 – the first time that the ANC took an in-depth look at rural development. Whether the government will pursue that position vigorously remains to be seen.

None of this is possible with a public service that is not geared to economic development. Richard Levin, director general of the Department of Public Service and Administration, has been remarkably frank on this matter (Levin, 2008). It is not only a matter of 'good governance', that preoccupation of economic policy-makers in the developed world. Much more, it is a matter of competent intervention to ensure economic advance. Since South Africa already has a developed first economy with substantial technological know-how, this translates into the need for intervention to release the productive potential of the rest of the population in the second economy or underdeveloped sectors: the townships and rural areas.

It is now evident that, although the government is stretching its spending to provide social grants to 16- to 18-year-olds, this is not a solution to our economic problems and is probably not sustainable. It is merely a palliative until a better answer is found. A very sharp reminder that a better answer is needed came in the shock finding that South Africa is now 'the most unequal society in the world' (Bhorat & Van der Westhuizen, 2009). We must ensure that we do not succumb to the kind of fatalism that has swept over the rest of Africa, that nothing can be done short of international rescue.

A special responsibility therefore rests with our policy-makers and intellectuals to find a new paradigm that will take us out of the old orthodoxies in macroeconomic policy. These may have sustained our economy but have done little to redirect it to a solid growth path based on our substantial physical and human resource base. The fact is that all the improvements in social services have not adequately built a platform in skills and capabilities for further advance. Only the state has the capability to do that in a systematic and deliberate manner.

'No developmental state, no development'

Political sociologist Peter Evans, one of the early proponents of the developmental state concept, argues that there can be no development without the creation of a developmental state. However, 'translating this basic insight into concrete proposals for the construction of effective state institutions is anything but simple. There is no fixed, universal model for how to build a developmental state … Only a flexible, creative process of exploration and experimentation that pays careful attention to local institutional starting points will succeed' (Evans, 2009).

Evans's central message is that, in order to be 'developmental', a 21st-century developmental state must be a capability-enhancing state. Expanding the capabilities of the citizenry is not just a 'welfare' goal. It is the inescapable foundation for sustained growth in overall GDP. (Not that GDP is the main criterion. Evans follows Amartya Sen's proposition that growth of GDP per capita is not an end in itself, but a proxy for improvements in human wellbeing.) Priority lies with health and educational services, with water infrastructure close behind. Other essentials include public transportation. But he stresses that 'the administrative capacity to efficiently deliver collective goods and infrastructure has political foundations. Without accurate knowledge of what collective goods the citizenry needs and wants, states can invest vast resources but fail to enhance capabilities. Active democratic structures are necessary for effective economic action' (Evans, 2009).

Evans then asks, 'What kind of institutional arrangements will best enable societies to build the organisations and networks needed to generate new skills, new knowledge and ideas, and to diffuse and take advantage of these intangible assets? ... To be developmental, a state must perform at least two general roles. It must support a distribution of basic rights that gives individuals incentives to invest in their own capabilities ... At the same time the state must offer a programme of skilful social support for healthcare, education and other social arrangements' (Evans, 2009).

Richard Levin approaches the issue of enhancing capability rather differently (Levin & Masvanhise, 2009). In the context of a regressive global economic environment, he argues that a more focused approach is necessary to ensure that the public service delivers despite the scarcity of resources. The emphasis here is to develop a suitable operational model of government with 'innovative strategies and leadership' to 'redistribute state resources and government services in favour of poor and vulnerable communities'.

For South Africa this requires, as a key feature, 'the provision of a seamless system of government'. This should drive towards coordinated government with a leadership cadre in a framework 'which harmonises the systems, institutions and personnel management in national, sub-national and local domains of government'. The progressive transformation of the state focuses on 'organisations, systems, people and culture' and must engage all sectors of society to arrive at a shared set of values that will 'include a stronger focus on service delivery and ethics'.

A 'people-centred administration', according to Levin and Masvanhise, should require public servants to collaborate, as is set out in the draft Public Administration Management Bill, which creates a single public service with the following objectives: alignment of institutions, responsive service delivery, a single window, a shared vision, sound employment practices and an easy mobility between the spheres of government.

Presumably Evans would argue that an effective public service is a necessary, but not sufficient, condition for an effective developmental state: the key requirement would still be to enhance the capabilities of the people as a whole. We would add that, in the South African situation, it also must enhance productive activity to overcome joblessness.

The global conjuncture

The global financial and economic crisis has sharpened our understanding of the nature of the world economic system. It has prompted serious reconsideration of the functioning of the system and the macroeconomic theories that guided financial policy in particular. Recent high-level meetings have agreed that the leading role of the United States has diminished significantly and that new emerging powers are creating a new balance of economic power.

It has also revealed that South Africa is a marginal player in the global economy, of little interest to traditional investors and trading partners. It is not an important part of the global production and value-adding chains. Sympathy for poverty does not lead to better economic relations, and we seem powerless to do anything about unfair trade relations other than offer mild rebukes to the recalcitrant North.

The new role of China as a world power and the growing economic strength of India and Brazil do offer some alternatives for Africa, but these relations must be subject to careful scrutiny, so that the principle of 'mutual benefit' rules. In the end, our salvation must lie in harnessing our own resources for our own benefit.

Constraints to advancement

One of the most serious impediments has been the iron grip of macroeconomic orthodoxy under the IMF and World Bank.

Many of our policy-makers and intellectuals have been captured and have lost their critical faculty. In addition, the policies of most other international agencies are weighted in favour of neoliberalism and require compliance from the state.

The structure of our economy will have to change in order to displace rent-seeking by value creation. In too many instances, the post-apartheid state has also become a vehicle for rent-seeking, leading to serious distortions.

While the apartheid state did tax the gold mining industry quite heavily – using the revenues to build state enterprises like Iscor, Sasol, Foskor and the rest – it did not actually direct the private sector into industrial projects. The huge profits made in the mining industry in earlier decades were not invested in industry but sent abroad. Anglo American first moved its design offices to London and later its head office, indicating a clear intention to shift its focus away from South Africa and invest in Latin America and elsewhere. Even our major insurance corporations, such as Old Mutual, have moved to London.

A developmental state approach offers various remedies to these ideological and structural constraints. As indicated above, the state must have clarity of purpose, focus in its programmes and total commitment. The ideology of development must become hegemonic and accepted as essential for national renewal by the whole of society.

The state must assert its autonomy against business interests, penalise destructive conduct and reward good behaviour (Turok, 2009). Evans (2009) argues that the state must avoid 'capture' and 'be able to discipline entrepreneurial elites'. The private sector will have to be given far more direction by the state, partly with incentives and partly by exercising state power, as was the case with the Asian Tigers. The state must be willing and able to intervene selectively and effectively where there is market failure, by building its own capabilities and through appropriate planning.

If our present government is to attempt to encourage the private sector into industrial projects, it will have to introduce new kinds of state incentives, the provision of training and low-interest loans, and other mechanisms such as those used by the Asian Tigers to nurture infant industries and support productive enterprises (cf. Chang, 2008). One of our most neglected areas is agro-processing. While we have strong wine and fruit-processing industries, with considerable exports, the rest of our agricultural produce could be beneficiated much more, creating many labour-intensive small enterprises. The DTI's 2010 Industrial Policy Action Plan (IPAP2) has examined this approach in some detail. However, since the private sector has shown no appetite for investing in either small enterprises or the former homelands, the state will have to lead the way.

Land reform is another important vehicle for gaining the support of rural people and boosting value-creating productive activity. Land banks and cooperatives are important. Once rural development becomes a reality, it can lead to first-stage industrialisation through small enterprises.

Capitalist principles in the economy now include treating currencies as commodities, leading to speculative activity and gross financial instability. We need to consider steps to relate currencies in Africa to value in the real economy.

South Africa's public service and the developmental state

We need to understand and accept why we have too often not met our objectives in delivering quality services. The reasons vary in different areas. Amongst them are: lack of political will, inadequate leadership, management weaknesses, inappropriate institutional design and misaligned decision rights. The absence of a strong performance culture with effective rewards and sanctions has also played a part. – The Presidency, 2009

Is our present public service in a condition to support a developmental state? A critic has characterised the South African public service as an institution that does not *deliver* but *procures* services. The comment is perhaps overdrawn, but the evidence of widespread outsourcing is indeed substantial (Turok, 2008a:5).

Richard Levin (2008) argues that, 'in a developmental state, the government leads a strong, concerted drive for economic growth, ensuring the mobilisation of national resources towards developmental goals', and such a state is indispensable here, as the inherited social legacy 'will not be addressed through the operation of the market'. He then examines the capabilities of the South African state and finds it seriously deficient. The 1998 Presidential Review Commission already found that the system of governance was not working well, citing a lack of career paths, unsatisfactory performance management systems, a lack of synergy in skills development and many other structural weaknesses.

Levin mentions various other reports that have highlighted the fragmentation of service delivery caused by a 'silo-based approach', which led to duplication and wastage. The 'cluster approach' adopted by Cabinet provides only horizontal integration, whereas 'effective integration often requires coordinated action across the spheres of government'.

Management

Management capacity in the public service is still underdeveloped. Under apartheid, it served a limited population and had relatively high income-to-service ratios. The new government managed to retain some experienced public servants, but many lacked the skills and values required to drive a more developmental state. There is a high turnover of public service managers, and few directors general (heads of national departments) and heads of provincial departments have more than a couple of years' public service experience.

The South African public service is very complex and highly regulated. The Public Service Act and Regulations prescribe myriad procedures which most senior managers find difficult to comply with. New regulations about policies and procedures are received every month, and senior managers need to rely on legal advisers to ensure that they comply. Senior managers in all spheres of government also have to keep extensive records and complete dozens of reports to ensure compliance. This takes up a large portion of their time. A former municipal manager in the Cape Winelands District Municipality said he had to complete around thirty reports per month to national and provincial government departments. Clear records must be kept for every decision made, and spending is strictly regulated by the Public Finance Management Act. The effect of this substantial 'paper chase' is that public service is regulation-driven, not value-driven. Top personnel, who are seriously overworked, resort to hiring consultants for research, strategic planning and report writing. The consultants add vital capacity, but in the long run we need to establish some of that capacity within the senior management of the public service.

Directors general are often appointed from outside the department and for only a three-year term. They often change when a new minister takes over, and are still viewed as political appointees. The limited contracts and political appointments do not provide job security, and many senior managers migrate to the private sector.

Performance management systems are now mandatory for all managers in the public service. However, we seem reluctant to use these to discipline or remove incompetent people. The emphasis is on overcoming weaknesses, but unless the senior manager is committed to vigorous capacity development in his or her department, mediocrity is tolerated. In many parts of the public service, productivity, morale and integrity are deficient. White-collar crime – such as the abuse of government vehicles and equipment and the petty theft of office supplies – is not uncommon.

In spite of improvements to intergovernmental relations, most departments still work in 'silos' with little strategic insight or cooperation with other departments to achieve development goals.

Political powers

Ministers and MECs (provincial ministers: members of the executive council) account to Parliament and the provincial legislature as well as the Cabinet. They direct and supervise the work of departments on behalf of the executive. But the actual management of departmental appointments, budgets and implementation is the responsibility of the heads of department. In too many cases, there is direct political interference in appointments and decision-making. Ministers and MECs seem unable to distinguish between laying down policy and managing implementation. Ministers are not specifically accountable for financial and human resource management, but their interference can seriously hamper the ability of senior managers to deliver. Where there are allegations of corruption or mismanagement, it is usually managers who face the consequences, while the Minister may just move on.

Senior managers find it difficult to resist politically motivated instructions even when they may be against legal opinion. They risk being marginalised, redeployed or facing 'constructive dismissal', an anodyne term for having one's life made impossible. In the Western Cape, senior provincial managers left the public service or were demoted after the Erasmus Commission investigation found that they had accepted political orders even after they had alerted their principals that the orders might not comply with the law.

It may not be unfair to say that mediocrity is common in our public service, and that there is a serious deficiency in professional skills and outcomes-driven management.

Skills and capacity development

In India, public servants complete an entrance exam before starting work. Many countries have a stepped system where public servants progressively build on their qualifications through tertiary institutions. In South Africa, there is no coherent capacity-development programme for public servants. Training is carried out by a variety of institutions. Many senior public servants take university courses in public management and administration, but the curriculum is determined by the university not the public service. Public servants also do a host of in-service training courses. The Public Administration, Leadership and Management Academy (PALAMA) is an important delivery agency. Most courses are outsourced to consultants and private agencies under PALAMA supervision. Many are tailor-made, but few require participants to be examined or adequately assessed. Some courses are run in the departments by departmental or provincial government academies or private agencies. At the local government level, training is done by the Local Government Sector Training Authority (LG-SETA), the Local Government Training Academy, the South African Local Government Association (SALGA) and the Department of Cooperative Governance and Traditional Affairs. The trainers are seldom experienced practitioners, and managers find many courses to be below their level of expertise.

A large amount of funding is spent on training public servants, but our approach appears to be scattered and poorly directed. An overall strategy for training needs to be developed that will help build the strategic and technical capacity needed to drive the developmental state. A progressive approach is needed that leads to proper qualifications, high-quality courses, assessment and improved competence of trainers.

Raisibe Morathi, a former senior official in the Presidency responsible for the Joint Initiative on Priority Skills Acquisition

(JIPSA), holds that the shortage of skills is 'at the nerve centre of transformation'. The costs of skills development are high, and 'none of the current efforts for skills development are catching up with the challenge.' Even though the public sector gives preference to black candidates, it does not ensure that they are competent to do the job. She also argues that the education system is failing, that Broad-Based Black Economic Empowerment (BBBEE) scorecards have become 'a comfortable compliance-and-numbers game' and that other administrative measures fail to produce good results. Morathi also argues that employment equity targets are too ambitious and that we would be better served by more focus on specialist skills such as accounting, engineering and medicine. The state should be far more focused on skills generation and not be afraid to outsource management 'in most of the critical public services, such as schools and hospitals'. Finally, she says that the government should create better incentives to increase training and skills development, without which 'we will have perpetuated a high entry barrier for skills development and denied our children better opportunities' (Morathi, 2009).

Coordination

The Constitution states that 'the national, provincial and local spheres are distinctive, interdependent and interrelated'. It requires the spheres to provide 'effective, transparent, accountable and coherent government for the Republic as a whole'. These requirements are only partially met by the President's Coordinating Council, which includes the President, key Cabinet members, premiers and SALGA. Nor are the problems overcome by the MINMECs, which bring together ministers and their provincial counterparts.

This leads Levin (2008) to advocate the creation of a single public service to embrace the national, provincial and local public services and enable the 'fundamental transformation of the administrative state apparatuses'. His advocacy of a single public service should not be seen as a stand-alone issue, but as a reflection of widespread frustration at the national level with the laborious way the state operates, given the separation of powers between national, provincial and local spheres. My own experience with housing provision bears this out. The national Department of Human Settlements provides funding to the provinces for housing, which is then supposed to be passed on to the municipalities to provide informal settlements and other housing. The only power that then resides with national government is to persuade the other spheres to follow national policy, but there are no enforcement provisions. National policy can be, and often is, ignored. In theory, the national department could then refuse further funding, but this is an extreme measure that could cause a constitutional crisis.

If we are to move to a developmental state, this will have to change. A balance must be struck within a strong state system that would enable public representatives to give direction throughout the system, while retaining within the public service the operational powers to implement such policies.

Levin also discusses the existing state planning system based on the medium-term strategic framework (MTSF), the five-year plan based on the ANC's election manifesto. But, he states, the country has not to date produced a long-term national development plan. This is obviously the gap that the National Planning Commission is designed to fill. He concludes that 'the achievement of a developmental state must ultimately be measured by its capacity to promote shared, sustainable, employment-generating development and growth in an environment that respects and nurtures democracy and democratic institutions.'

The developmental state and transformation
Many of our senior managers are well educated, with degrees,

postgraduate qualifications and substantial on-the-job training. Nevertheless, it is also the case that the transformation of our public service and other state institutions, in line with the requirements of race- and gender-based affirmative action, has led to the rapid promotion of staff with inadequate skills and experience. Given the legacy of Bantu Education, with the often poor quality of teachers and poor facilities at schools, and the obstacles to higher-level employment, it is hardly surprising that some managers are underqualified. This problem is aggravated by the complexity of our state system and the advanced character of our economy and social organisation.

There is also the problem of working for a government that has yet to formulate clearly its development objectives in a form that can be effectively translated into action by the public service. The Cabinet seems to put forward too many priorities, which are not related causally. The Ministers of Trade and Industry and of Economic Development have both made policy pronouncements. Excellent as these may be, it is not sufficiently clear which priority will lead the rest. This poses a problem for public servants, who need to be very clear on this in order to organise their own areas of responsibilities.

A further difficulty arises from the fact that the government is pursuing a transformation agenda. A public servant would be entitled to ask what it is that we are transforming into. What kind of society is envisaged, and what kind of state? In particular, what is the role of the state in the economy? There is intense debate about this internationally. States run by communist parties feature a command economy. In social-democratic states, state intervention takes a more indirect form. As we have seen above, the state was central in the 'Asian Tiger' economies. But the transformation debate is not only about economic policy. A transformation agenda raises a whole range of concerns about values and ethics. Thabo Mbeki gave some signals about this when he was president, when he spoke about conspicuous consumption and greed. There are also issues around the 'rainbow nation', gender equity, *ubuntu* and other traditional values. Perhaps most important of all is the Freedom Charter's declaration that 'South Africa belongs to all who live in it,' which implies a non-racial society where all have equal rights to the fruits of our labour and resources. How does the public service respond to this challenge in practice? Clearly the conventional training provided by some institutions is insufficient for a country facing our enormous challenges.

In an important UK study, Ivan Turok and Peter Taylor (2006) looked at skills enhancement in the fields of urban regeneration and planning. They argue that 'broader skills and attributes are required to deliver a more holistic and sustainable approach to development,' including an appreciation for the linked environmental, social and economic dimensions of urban change. Professionals working in separate disciplines and institutions need a 'proactive involvement [to identify] local development opportunities'. Because 'underlying issues extend beyond technical and procedural skills', a new skills agenda is needed (Turok & Taylor, 2006).

A new approach should include (Turok & Taylor, 2006):

- *strategic skills* to help initiate and promote change, including leadership, lateral thinking and sound judgment;
- *process skills* to enable change to occur … [including] communication and negotiation skills, and attributes such as being adaptable, flexible and understanding;
- *practical skills* [which] contribute to the successful day-to-day running of an initiative. They include writing funding proposals, developing action plans, managing projects and maintaining good administrative projects.

The study concludes with a research finding on improving the capabilities of practitioners for the delivery of higher outcomes:

'The single most important means of learning regeneration skills is from observing what other people do. This practical experience appears to be valued more highly than formal education or training courses.' This is not to undervalue other forms of learning, but it reinforces the importance of creating opportunities for practical work with people in other places. Where new challenges await the public service, training has to be broad and practical, with much scope for lateral thinking, rather than rote learning. This message seems to be particularly relevant to present challenges in South Africa.

Even more important is that the political leadership has to give far more attention to infusing top public servants with their vision for the future and encouraging them to actively further that vision. During the years of struggle, there were no doubts about the cause people were fighting for. Have we the same sense of purpose now? And does the public service share that purpose? Does the notion of a developmental state offer a vision of participatory democracy in which citizens participate in political decision-making, economic activity and every area of social life?

What to do?

The central practical task in South Africa lies in rebuilding our public service around a new developmental ethos. In the words of Peter Evans (2009): 'Without competent, coherent public bureaucracies, capability-expanding public services will not be delivered.' But he warns that form is not enough: 'The temptation will be to build an institutional frame that is politically expedient but ducks the difficulties of delivering capability expansion – resulting in a state that calls itself developmental but undermines both growth and wellbeing.'

Policy-makers and intellectuals must study the work of critics in developed countries as well as the work of civil society and pro-poor NGOs. The universities can play an important role in overcoming economic conservatism. Political parties and other political institutions must be energised by a development agenda. Policy-makers and intellectuals must remove the blinkers of globalisation and formulate new, anti-neoliberal policies. The present paradigm must be supplanted by democratic developmentalism.

We need new analyses that emphasise the liberating role of accumulation through technological capabilities rather than the traditional focus on capital accumulation and mechanical notions of growth. We must focus on phasing in value-creating economic activity in a step-by-step manner, building not on illusory and unrealistic proposals, but on existing capabilities. Planning is vital.

There are new emerging powers in the world with an interest in investing in Africa and building its productive capabilities. Those states that have begun to shift in this direction should become the centres for new thinking and new policies and lead the way for the renewal of Africa. Their interventions should be based on the principle of 'mutual benefit' and not on aid. The aim should be for Africa to join international chains of value-creating productive enterprise and lift the continent out of its marginalisation. Africa could become an important area of economic growth if the necessary investment is made by the emerging powers. This process has started but is at a very early stage.

There is also an opportunity to make substantial advances in the area of green technology, linked to development programmes. This is, in any case, essential if Africa is to counter the disaster of climate change.

We close with the final words of Peter Evans's essay:

'If a 21st-century developmental state can promise a combination of high growth, broad-based employment expansion and a lighter ecological footprint, it's worth the prodigious effort required to create it.'

Sources

Bhorat, Haroon & Carlene Van der Westhuizen (2009). 'Poverty, inequality and the nature of economic growth in South Africa'. Briefing to Parliament, October 2009. Cape Town: Development Policy Research Unit, University of Cape Town. Available from www.pmg.org.za/files/docs/091008poverty.ppt; accessed 22 December 2010.

Chang, Ha-Joon (2008). 'South Africa paralysed by caution', in *New Agenda: South African Journal of Social and Economic Policy*, Issue 31, 3rd Quarter: pp 6–11.

Evans, Peter B. (2009). 'Constructing the 21st century developmental state: potentialities and pitfalls', in *New Agenda: South African Journal of Social and Economic Policy*, Issue 36, Fourth Quarter.

Levin, Richard (2008). 'Public service capacity and organisation', in Turok, Ben (ed.) (2008), *Wealth doesn't trickle down: the case for a developmental state in South Africa*. Cape Town: New Agenda.

Levin, Richard & Wongiwe Masvanhise (2009). 'Leadership, governance and public policy in an era of global economic crisis'. International Association of Schools and Institutes of Administration (IASIA) Conference, Rio de Janeiro, 3–8 August.

Morathi, Raisibe (2009). 'Skills development in South Africa', in *New Agenda: South African Journal of Social and Economic Policy*, Issue 35, Third Quarter.

Turok, Ben (ed.) (2008). *Wealth doesn't trickle down: the case for a developmental state in South Africa*. Cape Town: New Agenda.

Turok, Ben (2008a). 'Is the developmental state really controversial?' in Turok, Ben (ed.) (2008), *Wealth doesn't trickle down: the case for a developmental state in South Africa*. Cape Town: New Agenda.

Turok, Ben (2008b). 'What is distinctive about a developmental state in South Africa?' in Turok, Ben (ed.), (2008), *Wealth doesn't trickle down: the case for a developmental state in South Africa*. Cape Town: New Agenda.

Turok, Ben (2009). 'Breaking out: the case for democratic developmentalism. Towards a Pan-African policy process'.???

Turok, Ivan & Peter Taylor (2006). 'A skills framework for regeneration and planning', in *Planning, Practice and Research*, 21(4):497–509.

Chapter 4

The Making of a Developmental State: Advice to Parliament

by Ha-Joon Chang

The author is a professor at the University of Cambridge and one of the world's leading development economists. He is the author of Kicking Away the Ladder: Development Strategy in Historical Perspective *(Anthem, 2002) and* Bad Samaritans: The Myth of Free Trade and the Secret History of Capitalism *(Random House, 2008). He presented this lecture to Members of Parliament in Cape Town on 11 May 2010.*

I'm very honoured to be here. My visits to South Africa seem to be correlated with the changes in political atmosphere. I came for the first time as a young academic back in 1991 when apartheid was ending. For a while I was coming here once or even twice a year. And then I didn't come between 2000 and 2005, largely on account of a report I wrote that was very critical of the market-based approach to industrial policy. For a while, I was persona non grata. In 2005, the DTI invited me again and I have been working informally with some people there. And finally I am speaking in Parliament – so it looks like we're moving in the right direction!

I am not going to mince my words. I think that the ANC government has basically wasted the last 15 years of opportunity. Okay, maybe in the first few years there was a case for being cautious, for establishing that you were staying within the international structures. But what have you been doing for the past ten years? Frankly, very little has changed in the economic life of ordinary South Africans. As I say this, I don't mean to undervalue what the government has achieved. From an outside observer's point of view, the social transformation is remarkable. When I came in 1991, black people couldn't even look at white people, and now they live as equals. That alone is a huge achievement.

But in terms of economic wellbeing, what have you really done? Yes, you built houses, built more roads, but as far as I can see, there has been very little change. Economic growth has been sluggish, inequalities persist and you boast the highest unemployment rate in the world. You have not lived up to expectations! No wonder people talk cynically about the 'cappuccino' society: brown masses at the bottom with white foam on top and a few sprinkles of chocolate.

Without fundamental transformation in the productive structure of the economy, it is no wonder that many people feel deeply dissatisfied with their daily existence. You have a disciplined ruling party which keeps a lid on this, but there is growing recognition that things can't go on like this forever. For this reason, there is increasing interest in the developmental state model associated with the East Asian economic miracle: aggressive state intervention directing investment to promote particular sectors, through trade protection, subsidies, regulation, state ownership and other means, brought about unprecedented growth and structural transformation.

It's not simply because I'm from that neighbourhood that I am positive about the experience. There were negative aspects as well, and I'll go into them later. But between the early 1950s and the 1980s, these countries had per capita growth of about 6 per cent per year. This means that their income doubled every 12 or 13 years. By the end of that 40-year period, their income was eight or nine times what it had been. Back in 1961, South

Africa's per capita income was $400 and South Korea's was $80. Today, what is the per capita income of South Africa – $3 000 or $4 000? South Korea's is $28 000. That kind of transformation is enormous, so it's natural that people are interested in this model. But there's a widespread – and understandable – scepticism about its feasibility in the South Africa context. Can this be done? Do we have the right conditions?

What I think about this issue has been published in a chapter called 'How to "do" a developmental state: Political, organisational, and human resource requirements for the developmental state', in *Constructing a Democratic Developmental State in South Africa: Potentials and Challenges*, edited by Omano Edigheji and recently published by HSRC Press. My talk today is based on that paper.

Learning from others

The classic definition of the developmental state is a state that derives political legitimacy from its record in economic development, which it tries to achieve mainly by the use of selective industrial policy, as seen in East Asia between the 1950s and 1980s.

If you define it in this way, there is no point in discussing the issue any further. Why bother? South Africa is not South Korea or Japan. End of story.

But I think it is still useful to think about these other experiences. When I read the autobiography of Nelson Mandela, is there any chance I could replicate the things that he has done? I don't have the courage, the integrity. I come from a different country and different context. So what is the point of me reading the book? If you think like that, there is no point in looking at anything else. And it is interesting that these people who say you cannot learn from Japan or South Korea think there is nothing wrong with copying everything from America!

Looking at other experiences can shake us from our usual

assumptions. The best example is Singapore. If you read the *Wall Street Journal* and *The Economist*, you only read about Singapore's free trade policy and its welcoming attitude to foreign investment. Which it has. But you will never be told the facts that all the land in the country is actually owned by the government; that the government housing corporation supplies 85 per cent of housing; that more than 20 per cent of national output is produced by state-owned enterprises; and that they have the most draconian forced-saving scheme in the world. People are forced to save a certain proportion of their income and are allowed to withdraw it only on special occasions: when they are getting married, going to university, and so on.

If economies were invented using standard economic theory – whether free market or Marxist – no one would invent Singapore. All the elements that are said to be incompatible sit together in one country. So what do we learn from that? Reality is often stranger than fiction: you really have to look at other experiences to figure out how to do things.

Looking at other experiences can also teach us who we are and exactly what conditions we are facing. You start to realise what South Africa's assets and problems are. Take the ANC. You may take it for granted, but other countries don't have a mass-based, well-organised, disciplined party, and this gives you a huge advantage.

Developmental state models

In the paper, I emphasise that there are many different models of a developmental state, and looking at this diversity of experience can tell you a lot about how to 'do' a developmental state.

The classic case has political hegemony by a nationalist interventionist state, with some kind of organisation within the government that plans, coordinates and implements detailed sectoral industrial policy. This could be a formal planning agency like in France or South Korea or a line ministry like the famous

MITI (Ministry of International Trade and Industry) in Japan.

This classic developmental model is not just an East Asian phenomenon. France had a very similar arrangement in the 1950s, 1960s and 1970s. So when people try to tell you that the developmental state is just for those weird people in East Asia who eat their rice with chopsticks, please don't believe them! I am sure there are a lot of people in this country who would like to become like France: well, the French did it this way.

Then there are different types of developmental state in other countries. The Scandinavian countries did use selective industrial policies, although some countries more than others. Basically, the government decides which are the strategic industries. 'Strategic' could be defined in many ways: for productivity growth, technological development, employment, export earnings. There is a misperception that strategic industry and selective industrial policies are all about high-tech industries. They are not. A lot of the East Asian countries promoted their textile sectors as the strategic industry – giving it subsidies, etc. – because they wanted to use it as a cash cow, to earn foreign exchange so that they could buy advanced machinery and technologies from abroad.

From very early on, the Scandinavian governments actively promoted research and development. Late in the 19th century, Sweden set up research institutes in the different industries and tried to promote technological development. The welfare state was part of this development strategy in the sense that it promoted industrial upgrading. In conventional free-market economics, a welfare state is supposed to be a bad thing – because it gives all those lazy poor people money and makes them even lazier. But when you use it well, it can actually promote structural change and productive growth. Giving workers some social insurance reduces their resistance to change. Why are the autoworkers in America so desperate to keep their industries alive, whatever it takes? Because they know that when they lose their jobs, their lives are finished. They don't even have money to go to the hospital. Of course, it's a painful process to have to change jobs, but in Europe, particularly in Scandinavia, at least people know they won't be thrown onto the scrapheap of history if their industry shuts down. So they are much more open to changes. This is why, despite the continent being much more interventionist, Europeans are generally more open to international trade. In America, people know that when they lose their job through foreign competition, it is the end of their productive life. In Europe it is not like that, especially in Scandinavia where welfare is very well designed.

Also, these countries used active labour market policies. The government provided retraining, help in job search, even – in the case of Sweden – housing subsidies to encourage people to go to areas where there were new jobs. Sweden also used what is known as a solidaristic wage policy, which means you pay equal wages for the same workers in different industries. Low-productivity industries were pushed out because, for example, the electrician you are using has to be paid the same as an electrician in the most productive enterprise in the country. So this not only promoted social solidarity but also structural economic change.

The United States is an interesting case. They tell us they developed through free trade and free markets and we all believe them. But look at their history. The so-called 'infant industry' argument – that governments in developing countries need to protect and nurture their young producers against competition from First World countries through protection subsidies and other means – was first invented by none other than the first Treasury Secretary of the United States, Alexander Hamilton. And between the 1830s and the Second World War, following Hamilton's lead, the United States maintained the highest level of protection in the world.

After the Second World War, the Americans subsequently

wound down this protection and other intervention because they were now the top dog and didn't really need it – but they still engaged in a range of support for industries. The American sociologist Fred Block has called this a 'developmental network state' as opposed to a 'developmental bureaucratic state'. It is less organised, less visible, less coordinated, but still there are various agencies within the government that promote technological progress and economic development. The most important pieces in this game are research and development funding and public procurement programmes for high-tech industries. Virtually all industries where Americans still have technological advantages are the industries developed through these R&D and procurement programmes. For example: the computer was developed for the US Army; semi-conductors were developed with funding from the US Navy; aircraft for the US Air Force. The list includes the Internet, drugs, genetic engineering, and so on.

It's come down a bit since the Cold War, and varies from year to year, but between 40 and 60 per cent of all research and development in the United States is financed by the federal government. In Japan, only 20 per cent is funded by the government. So which is the more interventionist economy? They are just intervening in different areas in different ways. The Americans' biggest triumph is to have convinced the rest of the world that America does not have an industrial policy, that America has no developmental state. Because then other countries, since the late 1990s – including my own South Korea – stupidly converted to neoliberalism, thinking that this was the global standard, this is what the Americans do. If we want to become like America, we need to dismantle our industrial policy!

Make your own history

How can we create a developmental state in South Africa? I will look at three issues: politics, organisation of the government and human resources. These are frequently the areas people raise against creating some kind of developmental state. They say that a developmental state requires some kind of dictatorship: 'Look at South Korea, look at Taiwan, look at Singapore. We can't do this without sacrificing democracy.' They say that all these developmental states required a very centralised, monolithic state structure, and a country with a federal structure or local autonomy or a high degree of diversity cannot, and should not, do that. They say these countries have fantastic bureaucrats with very high capabilities, but South Africa does not have those kinds of people, so we cannot do that.

So I am going to run through these arguments. Does adopting the developmental model mean rejecting democracy? Some East Asian developmental states were dictatorships. I spent the first 25 years of my life under military dictatorship. Taiwan, for over 40 years, was ruled by martial law. But even in the case of classic developmental states, there are countries like Japan and France. And if you widen the scope, you will find the Scandinavian countries, whose democratic credentials cannot be disputed. A developmental state doesn't need a dictatorship. This is an argument invented by people who don't like the developmental state.

I'm not trying to argue that politics don't matter. In the East Asian countries, the reason that economic development became so key to maintaining political legitimacy was precisely because a Scandinavian-style welfare state solution was very difficult to implement, given Cold War politics.

To say that politics affects the kind of developmental state you can build is not the same as saying you are stuck with whatever political landscape history has given you. We might think of the strong Gaullist developmental state as a natural product of French tradition dating back to Jean-Baptiste Colbert, the finance minister of Louis XIV, but this was a reinvention of a tradition that had been discarded for over a century. Yes, France had a centralising tradition, but by the time of the fall of

Napoleon, the French were fed up with very strong leaders. They deliberately built a political structure that made it difficult for strong leaders to emerge. If you look at French economic policy throughout the 19th and early 20th centuries, it was more liberal, more *laissez-faire*, than the British. But when de Gaulle came to power, he built a new coalition. He said that, by following a weak state model and *laissez-faire* economic policy, France had become a third-rate country. It had more or less lost all the wars it fought in the previous century, and he needed to put the country together. I'm not necessarily recommending this; my point is that you are not stuck with one political tradition that you can never change.

For another example, we think that the Scandinavian countries could build democracy and the welfare state quite easily because they have a great tradition of cooperation made possible by equal distribution of land and all kinds of historical reasons. But in the 1920s, Sweden had the worst industrial relations in the world: they lost the highest number of working days per worker due to industrial strikes. This was stabilised only in the late 1930s, when the capitalists and unions realised that this was the road to mutual destruction. In 1939, they signed an accord, a grand bargaining agreement. The labour unions stopped demanding that all means of production had to be nationalised, which was the standard union demand in the late 19th and early 20th centuries. In return, the capitalists would pay high taxes and build the workers' state.

You might think that Finland is a nice little country with 4.5 million people, and that they all must have lived happily together, holding hands and singing songs, for the last 2 000 years. Not at all. Finland has a very chequered history. For nearly 600 years, from the 13th century, it was a Swedish colony. Then in 1809, Sweden lost a war with Russia, and Finland became a Russian protectorate. After the Russian Revolution broke out, Finland declared independence, which was quickly followed by a civil war. It was a relatively short civil war, but tens of thousands were killed in a country of, at that time, 3 million people. Afterwards, the victorious right suppressed the basic political rights of the defeated left. Until 1944, when Finland was defeated in the Second World War as part of the Axis, communists could not vote in Finnish elections. It is only since the 1960s that Finns have come to terms with this and built a proportional political system. The point I'm trying to make is that, if you scratch the surface, these stereotypes – the cooperative Finns and the centralising French – are all wrong. As Karl Marx said, it's humans that make history, even though they might not be making it in a context of their own choosing.

Applying this insight to South Africa: on the positive side, you have a uniquely strong party base which enhances policy implementation capacity, and there are highly developed organisational vehicles that can be used for developmentalist projects, like the DBSA (Development Bank of Southern Africa), IDC (Industrial Development Corporation) and various state-owned enterprises. On the negative side, for a developing country you have energy and minerals conglomerates with unusually globalised links and capabilities, and so you have bigger problems to handle. I'm not saying you have to destroy these people, but you have to strike a deal with them and exactly how you will do that remains to be seen.

I'm not going to pretend that I can say anything useful to you. My knowledge of South Africa is very limited and some of it is outdated. I'm just trying to draw your attention to the fact that, given these positive and negative conditions, it is up to you – especially you people in politics – to make what you want to make. Even when I go to other countries, I tell people that, in the mid-1980s, Margaret Thatcher said that those who believed they would see black majority rule in South Africa one day were living in cloud-cuckoo land. You have proven her wrong, and you should prove these other people wrong who believe that

South Africa does not have the right political conditions to do anything useful.

The issue of organisation

The way you organise a developmental state depends on who you are, the structural constraints that you face and the choices and innovations you make. In the pure model, you see cases like South Korea or France, with powerful planning ministries orchestrating the activities of different ministries. But where you do not have that kind of set-up, you can use other vehicles. For example, Japan had a planning agency, but it was really an internal think tank: small, with no power. So the MITI had to take the leading role. Taiwan, with their industrial development board coordinating committee, had even less. It couldn't plan things the way the French or the Koreans could, but it still provided a coordinating function. The United States has sectoral agencies. So there are many different ways.

Thinking about this in the South African context, I would say, on the positive side, that there is a wide range of organisations that are potential ingredients for a developmental state. The DTI is in a position to play the pilot agency. I hear that you have set up a new planning ministry – although you may have the wrong minister. You have serious financial resources and analytical capacities in the DBSA and the IDC. You have a significant number of state-owned enterprises with an international standard of technological and business capabilities. There are quite a lot of elements available to you.

On the negative side, you have no control over the banking sector. In South Korea and Taiwan until the 1980s, all the banks were owned by the state. In Japan, some state-owned banks were part of the developmentalist regime, with a development bank, long-term finance, trade credit, and so on. But in this country, you don't have that. The finance industry here is too strong. I hear that now that the industrial capitalists are even revolting against it and have signed a document with the main unions. Personally, I think that is the kind of political alliance you need to build here – a 'real economic alliance' of the people who actually produce things. Also, when I did the industrial policy review in the 1990s, I saw there was a great weakness in agencies to promote research and development. Perhaps the situation has changed, but I don't think so. You have to do something about that. I have some suggestions, things that I believe are in the realm of political possibility: strengthening the Development Bank, establishing special-purpose banks under state ownership – banks for small and medium enterprises, export–import bank, agricultural bank, and so on – and also strengthening the research, development and support function of the state.

Human resources

People often say that, even if you manage to set up the developmental state politically, developing countries typically don't have the human resources, especially at the higher end, to run it properly. This is usually offered as common sense, but it is not true.

First of all, except for Japan, all the East Asian countries had – contrary to the prevailing myth – a rather low human capital base at the beginning of the post-war period. Despite apartheid policies, South Africa and Rhodesia had higher literacy rates in the late 1940s than South Korea. And reflecting this low level of human resources, South Korea was, up to the late 1960s and early 1970s, sending government officials to countries like Pakistan and the Philippines for extra training. So what 'exceptional human resources' are we talking about?

People then say, 'Well, maybe they had better economists.' But this couldn't be further from the truth. Economists were conspicuous by their absence in the East Asian development states. The Japanese economic bureaucracy was run by lawyers. Korea was similar until the 1970s, although it had more economists than Japan did. Taiwan was run by engineers, as is today's China. And what little economics they knew was of the wrong kind: Karl Marx, Friedrich List, Joseph Schumpeter. When you look at what these people did, you can see those influences. They never talked about 'getting the prices right', or free trade. It was all about capital accumulation, technological progress, labour discipline, mobilisation of surplus.

Reflecting on the South African case, I would argue that South Africa already has enough capable people to 'do' a developmental state. You think you don't because you don't want to do it. Which is not to say that everything is fine. The public–private salary gap leads to a draining of manpower from government, and the overly cautious policies of the last 15 years have failed to stretch the capability of the remaining people. You need to do something about these things. Existing officials need to be given additional training and more challenging tasks, while capable people should be retained and recruited through higher salaries and higher social status. But one word of caution: in trying to upgrade the economic bureaucracy, the country shouldn't get hung up on hiring more better-trained economists who, in my view, may be positively harmful for economic development. I'm not saying you should not hire any economists, but when people talk about government capabilities, they say we need more people with PhDs from MIT, more people with master's degrees from Oxford. I don't think that is how you going to get the right people for running a good developmental state.

To conclude, I would argue that there are many different ways to 'do' a developmental state, and each of these ways has different strengths and weaknesses – but you are going to have to find your own way. I am sorry that I have been too unkind to the ANC. I deliberately wanted to work you up so you would listen to me! I repeat that I do not know enough about local conditions to make concrete suggestions, but I hope what I have discussed here today has provided some food for thought for all of you.

Ha-Joon Chang's responses to questions

Defining development
In my view, we have to put the development of productive capabilities at the centre of this notion of development. It is not just about having resources. There is a reason why people are reluctant to call countries like Kuwait 'developed'. The fact is that Kuwait has a per capita income almost as high as that of Italy. They can extract resources by using other people's technology, but when the resources run out, what are they going to do? Conversely, when Germany's per capita income fell to something like 40 per cent of the pre-war level after the end of the Second World War – to the level of Peru and Mexico – no one suggested that Germany should be reclassified as a 'developing country'. They knew that Germans had the technology and organisational capabilities and the institutions to rebuild the economy, which they did in ten years.

Developing productive capabilities has to be at the centre of it, and then you have to add the humanist elements. Material wealth is important, but so is the way you share it and the kind of solidarity you have between members of society. But the definition of 'development' is itself part of this political project. Only you can define what you mean by development.

Defining a developmental state
It's true that I didn't offer a positive definition of a developmental state. In the paper itself, I broaden the definition to designate a state that deliberately tries to affect the course of economic development with policies that deliberately discriminate between different sectors. I am getting rid of the political condition, and, yes, this is unfaithful to the original concept. But concepts are there to serve us, not to enslave us. If it works, it works. I'm quite happy to be criticised for my excessive pragmatism.

China

We have never had a country like China. It's a country where people still work 13 hours a day for 364.5 days a year for a wage of $100. At the same time, they can build nuclear reactors and send a man into space. In the late 1980s, Thailand was booming and a lot of people thought it was doing well, but Thais had low wages – and that was it. They didn't have a space station!

I don't know where to begin talking about China, but as a good Korean I would probably say I'm not convinced that a world dominated by the Chinese is any better than a world dominated by the Americans. At the moment, they are working as a positive force. They provide competition against the Americans and they don't attach conditions on their loans. But in the long run, I'm not so sure.

Land reform

I have two things to say. First, how do you destroy a class that is structurally against industrialisation, i.e. the landlords? Don't forget that the United Sates had to fight a civil war to resolve that issue. The Southern landowners and slaveowners were totally against those policies. They very rationally argued that they could sell their tobacco to Europe and import things from Europe that were better and cheaper, so why should they subsidise Yankee manufactures? So do you have to fight a war over that?

Secondly, land reform establishes a more equal society. According to historical data, Japan was more unequal than America before the Second World War, mainly on account of very unequal land distribution. That problem was eliminated and it created solidarity and performed a very positive function. Now the question is whether trying to do something like this in South Africa is going to create more problems than benefits. In my view, there is nothing in this world that is only positive or only negative. Yes, land reform creates some negative consequences, and you might have more negative than positive consequences, depending on how you do it. But frankly, that's your job. You are politicians. Economists are not qualified to answer a question like this. How do you forge an alliance or a certain agenda that maximises benefits and minimises the cost? But when you do it well, the benefit is clear.

The price of social peace
I admire the ANC and the South African people for having been very disciplined in this process. If we had had a similar situation in South Korea, there would have been a bloodbath. Koreans are very impatient. So I really admire you for that, but even within that general framework of keeping social peace, you could have pushed it further. I don't think you have done enough of that.

Can the DBSA and IDC work for development?
Yes, but you have to make them do it. You're the parliamentarians. And if you cannot do it, what is the point of having a democracy?

The model for South Africa
I don't want to stretch myself too far, but given your strong trade unions and broad resource base, I think that Scandinavia would be a better example for you than East Asia. East Asia didn't have natural resources, so they had to squeeze the workers. Scandinavia did – forestry, iron ore, fisheries – and they had some room to manoeuvre. But please don't follow any one model or any single country slavishly. You can learn things from everywhere – including the negative lessons.

State capacity
If a state cannot collect a basic amount of taxes or cannot force companies to abide by regulations, then there is a problem. Do you think that this country has that problem? You collect a huge amount of taxes and such capabilities are not easy to come by. You have all these levers that you are not using.

Labour market

You might look down on the Koreans and Taiwanese for having repressed workers, but in those countries almost everyone who wants a job has a job. Yes: badly paid, beaten up by the foreman – in case of female workers, being sexually abused by the men on the shop floor. But at least the people have jobs.

Here, half the people are not working. What are you going to do about that? For those people, what is the point of all those nice labour laws? I am not saying that you should therefore change your labour laws to create more jobs. But I have a feeling that this country is not taking the unemployment problem seriously. You have one of the highest official unemployment rates in world. It is a national shame, just as it was a national shame for South Korea to have the longest working hours in the world. So please don't get me wrong. I want you to pay more attention to this issue.

Ben Turok: That was as controversial and stimulating as I had hoped. By way of summing up, I think Professor Chang has left us with four main points:

1. A developmental state is one that deliberately does something – and the word 'deliberately' is key. And it sets out an agenda that is understood and accepted nationally.

2. We cannot be complacent. We cannot, after 16 years of democracy, sit back and say we have done very well and just continue as before. His closing remark on unemployment was very strong and I think we need to take it very seriously.

3. 'We could have done more' is quite a contentious statement. I wonder what Professor Chang would have proposed for us if he had been in the first Cabinet in 1994. At some stage, we need to reflect on this: could we have done more? And what is the 'more' we should have done, and how?

4. Finally, and this is very important, he says: 'Don't follow other people. Work out your own salvation.' I take that very strongly.

I always find it very uncomfortable when we invite economists like the Harvard Group to come and tell us what to do. Professor Chang was invited to tell us about the experiences of other countries, but not to teach us a model that we must follow. I would urge that we in Parliament must put on our thinking caps every day to work out our own destiny. We can do this as South Africa. If we can build our own nuclear bomb, why can't we get rid of unemployment?

Chapter 5
Finance for Development: Lessons From Brazil
by João Carlos Ferraz

The author is director of research, corporate planning and risk management at the Brazilian Development Bank (BNDES). This chapter is based on his presentation to a workshop on 'Sourcing finance for development: Prospects for economic transformation', held in Pretoria on 21 April 2010. The workshop was hosted by New Agenda and the Human Sciences Research Council (HSRC) with cooperation from the Friedrich-Ebert-Stiftung.

It seems appropriate to place the discussion of financing for development in the broader context of the era and world we are living in. Then I will give you an idea of what is happening in Brazil and the role of the Brazilian Development Bank (BNDES: Banco Nacional de Desenvolvimento Economico e Social), and I will comment on policies that are being implemented in the country.

Issues for development
In Brazil, I would argue, there are four main issues. First, for the long term – and in the post-crisis context – financing for development will involve both more state resources and more market resources. The increase in market resourcing will become clear when I show you what BNDES has done in the recent past.

The second point concerns the developmental state. Peter Evans, the American sociologist, states that without a developmental state there is no development. Developmentalism in the 21st century is not the same as it was in the middle of the 20th century. In the 21st century, there are development challenges in South Africa, but there are also 21st-century development challenges for Japan and for the US. Small country, big country – it doesn't matter.

In my definition, a developmental state would focus on building up competencies and inducing the creation of more and better jobs in the economy. The 'more' means absorption or quantity, and 'better' would indicate that what we are doing is improving the quality of life. Maybe I've summarised too much, but that is more or less what I perceive. This understanding of a developmental state is not derived from concepts and hypotheses. It is a normative statement.

The third point is that a public development bank is an essential vehicle to that end. To be effective, it must have the necessary resources, the financing tools, the lines of credit. And not only resources in terms of funding, but also the technical capabilities for risk management, evaluation, etc.

And fourthly, the most important issue is to maintain close relationships with stakeholders, especially with the Treasury. But it is a close two-way relationship, providing funding on one side and dividends on the other. BNDES helps on the fiscal side as well. This is very important, because it is a public institution.

The world we live in

I will mention a few of my concerns in this world of uncertainties we are living in.

One is the question of where democracy and citizen participation is going. Is it only through political parties? The concept must be larger than just 'open societies'. The NGO phenomenon is very important but its representation is not clear.

Secondly, after 1989 and the fall of the Berlin Wall, the world moved into a situation of unipolar international power and now we're moving towards a multipolar state of affairs. It's not clear whether this will happen in a negotiated way or through conflict.

Then there is climate change. When this current trajectory will reverse, we don't know.

Fourth is role of the state. In the last two years, we have seen states doing things that, six months before the crisis, they would never have dreamed of. But this legitimacy is still not ensured. The new space that the state is taking is not consolidated yet. We're trying things out.

The fifth point concerns me very much and is related to competition and technical progress. We are in a period of slow growth in the near future, but technical progress has not stopped, and all countries and firms are exploring for markets. Nations and corporations will battle fiercely over the generation, distribution and appropriation of wealth. This is going to be horrible and it will call for a new discussion of 'national interest' and what that means.

The last point is that growth is in check. I come from a country that was in crisis more or less from 1978 until 1994. In 1982, there was the debt crisis. It was a long process. It takes a long time for things to become normal – and they do not *go back*. When they say that Spain will need five years to 'go back' to where it was, well, it is not going to be to where it was. We compare things with funny quantitative indicators like growth and GDP, but things change and – most important – countries differ. Take four countries affected by the current crisis: China, Hungary, the US and South Africa. What happened in the crisis, and how it has developed for each of them, is completely different.

The commodities debate
South Africa's economy is commodity-based, just like Brazil's. We are going through a period of increases in the prices of commodities, and world imports are increasing as well. Before

the crisis, commodity prices were rising. And then the crisis came, but still the commodities are playing in our favour. This brings back the Argentine economist Raúl Prebisch's observation from fifty years ago, that terms of trade would indicate declining benefits to commodity-exporting peripheral economies. Asia is the source of demand and maybe this demand pressure will continue – but there is a lot of discussion.

Should we go with commodities? Should we not?

The arguments against say we will be stuck with all these millions of tons of minerals and ore, and there will be a dual structure, and over-specialisation, and the 'Dutch disease' that affects the macro side and the exchange rate, and depletion of the environment with these industries. And then there is the mentality of the Chinese. I had meetings in China last year, and all the different banks there had Brazil on their minds: 'You provide raw materials and we process. If you want, we can do the investment, we can finance. Of course we'll produce and provide the machinery. And if you need, we'll provide the labour force as well!' This is what they're doing in Angola and other countries. So it's very clear the role that Brazil plays.

There are also arguments in favour of commodity exports. First, the mining industry of ten years ago and that of now are different animals. The context of competition is completely different.

The second argument I call 'the nature of nature'. When the first Portuguese arrived in Brazil, he said 'it's very easy; nature provides everything.' But it's not true. Brazil is the top orange juice and soya producer, but behind this is a lot of public agriculture research that was done to develop these species. The amount of knowledge production in the production chains associated with the natural resources sector is amazing.

The third point is the size and diversity of the resources sector. Consider Petrobras (a publicly-traded energy company; the Brazilian government is its largest shareholder). The oil in

Brazil is not like the oil in Saudi Arabia or in Venezuela. Oil in Brazil is 3 000 metres below the seabed, but Petrobras is on an investment drive. If you include all of Petrobras's suppliers, it is responsible for 26 per cent of formal jobs in Brazil and $35 billion of procurement every year.

Then comes the last point: down with determinism! Countries and societies make and implement choices. The US was developed on the basis of natural resources. In Venezuela – and this was true long before Chavez – the people believe that the oil is there to provide for them.

Even though we talk a lot about China being the source of demand, we should look where the consumption is. The US, Europe and Japan are the markets that count. The real aggregate demand in private consumption is there. We know that China is going to keep the prices of our commodities high, but we should not forget that the market is in the developed countries.

Brazil's situation
Let's look quickly at Brazil's situation in terms of assets, challenges and growth trends.

Assets
We have been through a very long process of uncertainty, but now we can say there is political and institutional stability. This is so important for a country.

We have a complex and diversified economic base and a lean private sector. As the world changes, everything that was negative in Brazil is now becoming positive. Our private sector has complete disdain for high levels of debt because of the bad period we went through during the 1980s. The country struggled for many years to fight serious inflation, which ran to 30 to 40 per cent a month. Now we have a very conservative central bank and the regulation of the financial sector is very strict. After the crisis, Brazil doesn't need to put any of this in place. What happened in the US – the sub-prime market and no regulation – would never happen in Brazil.

Challenges

Our challenges include:

Insufficient infrastructure. The extent of paved roads is low, only 212 000 kilometres, with 1.5 million kilometres unpaved. Russia, which has twice the area of Brazil, has 755 000 kilometre of paved roads. India, about one third our size, has 1.57 million kilometres of paved roads. The railways are even worse.

Innovation capabilities. The private sector's commitment to innovation is ridiculous. Germany spends 2.6 per cent on research and development over sales investment. Brazil spends 0.6 per cent.

Education crisis. In an international proficiency test of middle school students in mathematics, Brazil came in third-to-last place.

Opportunities for social mobility. Brazil had the record of being the worst in terms of inequality. In 2002, the Gini coefficient was 0.59, and there was a trend of decreasing inequality. Brazil experienced an economic inclusion process, an increase in the mass market, that was very good for production.

Growth trends

Brazil has travelled a long and winding road towards sustainable growth. From 1998 to 2002 the annual growth rate of GDP was 1.7 per cent. From 2002 to 2008 it was 4.2 per cent. And then came the crisis, and we are projecting that for the next five years growth will be around 5.5 per cent. Growth is 'on' in Brazil. We haven't had that for the past 35 years. In the early 1990s, everyone would manage their personal accounts every day in order not to be hit by inflation. The notion that you can now extend your horizon of investment is still something odd for us.

Economic growth before the crisis was ideal. There was social inclusion. GDP was growing. Employment, investment and productivity were all growing. A magic moment that will never come back!

During the crisis, there was a socioeconomic inclusion process taking place – thanks to social policies like the *Bolsa Familia*, a conditional income transfer programme for families, and increases in the real minimal wage – and there was growth. There was a deliberate policy to keep consumption up. For instance, there was a temporary tax reduction on durable goods. So consumption held.

In the export sector, more than 50 per cent of the drop in industrial production came from losses in exports of manufacturing goods.

Investment as a per centage of GDP is the figure we struggle with at BNDES. In 2008, it was increasing as fast as China's, above 15 per cent. In industrial policy, we projected we would get to 21 per cent in 2010. Well, we will be lucky if we get to the same position this year that we had in 2008. Now our struggle is to move this to 23 per cent in 2014. This is the price of the crisis – and we are a country that did not suffer much.

Crisis management

In the short term, what was the role of the state in managing the crisis? First, there was already strong financial regulation, so we did not have liquidity problems. Second, the central bank injected liquidity in the banking system by cutting down our reserve requirement – the level of their deposits that the banks cannot touch. These have been very high in Brazil.

All the liquidity that was pumped into American banks did not immediately turn into loans. I talked to a former student of mine, who is head economist at a bank. He said that the banks will only look at the Basel Index (an international regulation on banking governance), not market share. But then he said, 'I'm taking off my hat as the chief economist: It's time for the public banks to move. The private banks will start to provide loans again once they start to lose their market share.' So that is what we did.

From September 2008 to January 2010, credit growth was sustained by private banks (10 per cent), while BNDES pumped in 37 per cent. Behind this were two loans from the Treasury to BNDES, one of US$60 billion in December 2008 and then $40 billion later. The message from the Finance Minister was this: 'Ladies and gentlemen of the corporate sector who are interested in financing investment: *there is no credit crunch in this country.* You can invest.' In terms of policy, this was very important.

The next strategy was an equalisation programme. In discussions with the finance ministry we assessed that the economy was beginning to stabilise in April 2009. Every sign was that the worst had passed. We already had begun to withdraw the incentives for consumption, and now it was time to boost investment. The finance ministry set up an equalisation programme with an initial value of $25 billion. Equalisation meant that interest rates between 10 and 13 per cent would decrease to 4.5 and 7 per cent. As the minister announced, it was really an interest rate of zero.

BNDES's daily disbursement for capital goods acquisition is an interesting indicator here. It does this as a second tier through the banking industry. Most of the trucks in Brazil are bought through the banks with BNDES finance. In September 2008, disbursement was at a peak of around $85 million. By July 2009, the daily disbursement was at $33 million dollars and very concentrated. Only the big firms were taking it. The equalisation programme was announced then, and it just took off. In March 2010, it was around $122 million.

So there you have it: analysis, action and reaction. It was very successful. Over time, disbursement became de-concentrated, indicating that the investment was spreading out.

Of course, public debt is a concern, but we are very much

in control. These policies cost us 1.2 per cent of GDP, which is much lower than what has been done elsewhere. In terms of net debt, we were at 43.4 per cent of GDP in 2009, with 42 per cent projected for 2010. In comparison, public sector debt in the US, Germany and Japan was projected at 66.8 per cent, 76.2 per cent and 115 per cent, respectively, for 2010. Because Brazil was already conservative, we had room to manoeuvre.

Long-term investment

Then there are the long-term investment policies in science and technology, education, health, housing, productive or industrial development and infrastructure. Most of them are not just on the drawing board anymore. They have taken off in a growth acceleration programme known as PAC, which amounted to $300 billion between 2007 and 2010.

In 2007 we were criticised because we could not fulfil the budget, could not deliver. It was very difficult to get started. The state machinery for big projects was rusty. The environment ministry, the roads department, the city council ... They didn't have projects, didn't know how to run an investment drive. I thought it was not going to work. In October 2008, the Chinese announced a $600 billion investment programme for infrastructure. I went to China – and I thought they must be another species! One of their specialists said the reason was very simple: China has been growing for the past 20 or 25 years. They've had a long investment drive and filing cabinets full of projects.

The persistence of policy over time is so important for development and growth. It is crucial to keep these as national *state* policies, and not as *government* policies. BNDES is very important because it finances the private sector associated with these investments. The budget comes from the Brazilian budget, plus BNDES.

Industrial policy

Rather than 'industrial' policy, we talk about 'productive development' policy (PDP). This was made into a strong political priority.

All the relevant actors were involved. The executive secretariat of the PDP includes the ministry that is equivalent to your DTI, BNDES and the Minister of Finance – the guys who have the money. There is no industrial policy without the finance ministry. Who calculates how far you can go on tax incentives? The finance ministry. Who has the budget to provide loans? The finance ministry. So it is very important that there is participation by these different actors.

Brazil is complex, so the third factor is a systemic design. The policy configuration does not just aim at three or four sectors. For good projects, funding is ensured. But these 'good projects' must demonstrate that there will be returns: social, economic, in productivity and competitiveness. The policy has broad coverage, but it has very specific goals: investment, innovation, exports and small and medium firm size.

Two weeks ago we made a presentation to the President to explain why we will not fulfil our targets. He said that meeting the goals doesn't matter so much as persistence over time in one direction.

Finally, we have to look at management and implementation. Above 95 per cent of the proposed measures are operational. In ECLAC (Economic Commission for Latin America), we used to say that Latin Americans were very good at analysis and could design brilliant policies. But then … to implement? And to evaluate? So we made a great effort to develop management systems to escape from this curse of good analysis and bad implementation and evaluation. The challenge is to coordinate 500 civil servants and over 60 agencies, every one with different missions. This has to be long term. It is not something you do by snapping your fingers. General coordination is done by the ministerial council, which meets every six months for the ministers to give account of their projects. The executive secretariat organises programmes and each one has people responsible for it.

Turning to the achievements of our productive development policy, the first is again that it has achieved priority. We are now talking about investment and job creation. Even in negotiations with the private sector, we discuss where Brazilian industry is going.

The second is effectiveness: most measures are operational.

But the most important achievement is probably the private and public sector interaction in policy issues. Before, there were competitive forums where the public sector would sit on one side and the private sector on the other side. The private sector would come with its list: we want lower taxes and lower capital costs, etc. The civil servant from the DTI would take this, uncritically, and write a memo to the IDC (Industrial Development Corporation) that this particular sector wants a special credit line at a lower cost. Or he would write to the Revenue Services that this other sector wants tax reduced to some level.

Now it is very clear – more and more, as we keep repeating – that the private sector has to demonstrate what it wants and why it wants it. And then the decision is on the side of the public sector, because this is the allocation of public funds. There is no memo: we bring everything together and we evaluate the demands. Does this make sense? Does it fit with the budget? (Again, this is why the finance ministry is so integral.) And then we say yes or we say no.

The role of BNDES

In the 1950s and 1960s, BNDES was financing infrastructure through state-owned companies – for example, in steel or electricity. In the 1990s, BNDES carried out the privatisation of these companies. They sold what they had financed. And now they are financing the corporations that bought them and there are joint ventures between corporations and state-owned companies. For example, just yesterday there was a final bidding for a very large investment, worth $30 billion. The winner is a public–private joint venture and BNDES will be financing it.

As an institution, BNDES has to have the capacity to adapt and change. The new direction is a difficult one. It used to be that a factory could offer its equipment as a guarantee, but this is the era of 'financing the intangible': financial innovation, financial sustainability. How do you get a guarantee from that? And so, we are changing the credit system in order to value the intangible. The way that we analyse a project is being changed to take this into consideration. It's going to take many years.

Some facts and figures for BNDES. It is the main provider of long-term financing in Brazil, representing 13 per cent of fixed capital formation. It is a fully state-owned company under private law with institutional funding and 2 250 employees. Our disbursement is almost $70 billion per year. Our non-performing loans are very low, at 0.20 per cent. Our challenge now is to increase our equity to sustain all our assets.

It is important that BNDES has a wide range of instruments to finance development:

- direct and indirect operations: half our financing goes through the commercial banking system
- micro, small and medium enterprises: offering financing and guarantees
- export–import
- project finance
- equity investments
- non-refundable credit lines.

Within the same system, we have an investment bank. Our

portfolio is almost $50 billion. We have the largest assets with the investment banks. We sit on the boards of Petrobras and Electrobras and we sit on the board of the largest mining corporation. So we can actually play a strategic role in very large corporations in Brazil. When we finance a start-up company, we sit on that board. By doing this, BNDES is developing *with* the capital market. The Brazilian capital market is very developed in terms of governance, of the corporations being open and respecting minorities and all that. BNDES is an element of the push in this direction.

Economic implications
The Brazilian challenge is to evolve from growth to sustained development. We have successfully faced the crisis. The economy is going to grow, led by the internal market. Social and economic inclusion has taken a long time. We have to look at the capacity of the productive sector to provide there, and it is lagging. Then the finance ministry keeps looking at potential production to see if it will press inflation or not. There is a response through investment. Because of its expanding production capacity, BNDES is the partner of the Central Bank.

Investment has to grow ahead of GDP. Think about a country with such levels of inequality: it's horrible. Think about an accelerated process of economic inclusion. Think about the roads, think about the sewerage. The infrastructure that is needed to support the process of economic inclusion is very important – but so is the maturation time of infrastructure investment. The solution from the social inclusion approach takes longer than the solution driven by productive capacity. There is a tension here.

Now think of the problem of skills shortages. That will take even longer to build – even longer than a large dam or a port or a railway. Our plan for education is that, by 2022, the *average* Brazilian student in a middle school will be *average* in the international rankings. So if we keep on investing as we are doing *for 15 years* we will be ... average.

This is a tension that Brazilian society will have to learn to deal with – *because nirvana will not happen.* Our growth is unbalanced, and there is difference in the maturation times of investment in education and production for economic inclusion. This is why we need more investment, more savings and more opportunities.

From growth to development: what's needed?

First, we need permanent and effective investment policies. Then, in terms of financing development, we need more market support. It isn't just size that matters. We have a model that estimates the direct, indirect and income effect of jobs during an investment period. Of the $68.8 billion BNDES disbursed in 2009, this generated or maintained – not created – 4.5 million jobs during the investment period. But this cannot grow forever. It will tend to stabilise, and that's why market support needs to increase.

There are complaints about the $100 billion loans that BNDES was given in the past two years. That gross debt is important, and of course there is fiscal pressure. The Treasury will not provide another tranche of this size. Now we're starting to sit down with the banks. It's not BNDES that wants to increase. We want to know where the market is for financing. There are good opportunities for low-risk and high-return investment. This is very specific to Brazil. The state has done a lot and now we need market support for investment.

Socially, we need more and better jobs. In industry, we need innovation. Brazilian society must be prepared for the long term and we are not. When I go to a bank, I still try to negotiate. I carry my protective inflation behaviour from the past, and I do not think long term. I still want to have gains in the short term, and it's not possible to carry on like this.

Thoughts on development financing

In conclusion, when it comes to development financing, each nation has its own unique structure and aspirations, so these are singular institutions. BNDES is a singular institution, but some of its features may serve as food for thought:

- *Flexibility and capacity to adapt.*
- *Serving the public interest.* We are public servants in an insulated bureaucracy. BNDES would not be what it is if its 2 250 employees were not highly qualified and technically efficient.
- *Capacity to interact and negotiate* with stakeholders. There is negotiation all the time.
- *Ability to seize the opportunity,* to be in the right place at the right time and to assess conditions accurately.
- *Obsession.* In the history of BNDES, the period from 2007 to 2010 has been obsessed with this investment drive.
- *Political leadership* in the institution and in the country. We have a fortunate combination of leaders. We have a president at BNDES who has the mind of a development banker in the best sense. Our finance minister has a notion of where the country is going. And we have a President who also wants development; during his second term, he has maintained a very conservative central banker and a very progressive development banker.

Part Two

South Africa's Political Economy

Chapter 6
The Politics of Economics

I chose 'the politics of economics' as the title of this chapter because all economic policies are carried out in a context of politics. So, for example, whether the government adopts the RDP or GEAR or any international economic policy, it depends on the political context. Politics and economics are always interrelated. If you try and talk about economics without contextualising it in a political environment, you make a grave error. Following the release of the Green Paper on National Strategic Planning, COSATU made a very strong statement about the document and about the neglect of Ebrahim Patel as Minister of Economic Development. COSATU took a political position, not an economic position, because they feel we are facing an environment in which certain kinds of policy choices are going to have to be made. But those policy choices are not only made by economic criteria; they are made, above all, by political criteria. This is why want I talk about the politics of economics, because very often it is the politics that determines the economics. But the economics also determines the politics, as I will explain.

After I gave a talk on the international crisis, and the South African response, to the South African Democratic Teachers' Union (SADTU) General Council in Johannesburg, I asked some of the officials present if they understood what I had said. Some were quite frank and answered no. They explained that there is very little education about economics in the trade union movement. The same holds true for the ANC. We have not taught economics in the ANC for years. When I joined the movement, we talked economics all the time, but over the past decade there has been very little education around economics in ANC branches.

So, to set the scene, we need to discuss two traditions in economic policy. The first tradition is based on the labour theory of value, which was developed by Adam Smith, although he is not often recognised as the first theorist of the labour theory of value. That is the one school of thought. The other tradition is price economics, based on the price of goods. Generally, we talk about supply and demand being the school of thought that deals with prices of goods.

The first school of thought was developed by Karl Marx into a very sophisticated theory. He wrote three huge volumes, called *Das Kapital* (Capital), in which he developed a labour theory of value to help explain and understand classes and class structures in society. When you understand the labour theory of value, you can see how classes relate to each other. When, on the other hand, you talk about price, supply and demand, you are talking about the free market system or free market capitalism. Capitalism is based on the idea of the market and supply and demand; according to the second school of thought these are the two issues that determine the price of commodities, and indeed everything else. This is the philosophy of the free market system, of neoliberalism in its modern form.

The question facing us is, how does the national labour movement relate to these two schools of thought? We relate to both schools of thought because we live in a world where both operate. To illustrate this idea, take the example of the price of bread.

How is the price of bread determined? Some will say it is determined by the market: people produce bread, take it to shops and people buy it. It is a matter of supply and demand: the suppliers, the distributors and the manufacturers produce the bread; you and I constitute demand because we decide if we are going to buy the bread or not and how much we are going to buy. If there is a shortage of bread the price tends to go up, and if there is an oversupply the price goes down. The theory of supply and demand says that when the supply of any good increases, then there is an abundance and the price will go down; but when there is a shortage, the demand is greater than the supply so the price goes up. It is like bargaining. That is what the theory of supply and demand tells us: when there is a huge supply of a particular good, like labour, then the price goes down, but when there is a labour shortage, the price of labour will go up.

In South Africa, large companies decide how many loaves of bread to manufacture. A market expert will say that if last week we only sold four million loaves, this week we will only produce three million loaves of bread. The company will manufacture the three million loaves of bread and distribute them to supermarkets. One supermarket may call and ask for more bread, and so the company will supply another one million loaves of bread. Oversupply leads to a lowering of the price, and a shortage leads to price increases.

What determines demand, and why should demand be limited? Demand is determined by the amount of money consumers have. If there is full unemployment in a country then people will buy as much bread as they need. If there is not full employment – and we have huge unemployment – then people are very careful about how they spend their money, and demand will fall because people cannot afford to buy the bread. In the first case, where there is lots of money, there is still a limit to how much bread any person will buy because you will buy only what you can eat. There is a limit to the amount of food needed, and most companies know that.

How do the manufacturers know what price to charge for the bread? Here we come to the other theory. The manufacturer says that if I charge R25 for a loaf of bread, people will not buy bread. So how do I decide the price? Is it only the demand that determines the price of my bread? The manufacturer will ask his accountant how much it costs to produce a loaf of bread. The accountant will count various costs – of the flour, the machinery, labour and profit for the manufacturer. There are four elements to the cost of the price of bread. The cost of flour is fixed because flour is sold on the market. The machinery costs a lot, but it is used for years to produce bread. Then there is the cost of labour. The accountant will decide that you need 20 or 100 workers, for example, to produce bread and then calculate how much of that labour goes into one loaf of bread. The fourth element is how much profit the company makes. The accountant reminds the manufacturer that he must make a profit or go out of business.

However, there are other factors involved. The cost of the flour depends on agriculture, on rainfall and other things. The cost of machinery is worked out in terms of what accountants call depreciation; when you buy a new machine, you pay so much, but as the machine gets used, there is a depreciation or reduction in its value. The cost of the machine is 'written off' over time.

Next we come to labour. Marx said that when you have a machine and you have flour and you have an employer, you still do not have a single loaf of bread. It is only when you add labour that you get a loaf of bread. The machine cannot produce the loaf of bread by itself. Machines do not produce on their own; it is a worker who works on a machine that makes the product, even if it is under the supervision of the boss. Marx's labour theory of value takes account of all that. The labour theory of value says that the flour and the machine have a certain value, but the labour also has a certain value because you have to pay the worker. What happens is magic. You have a machine, you have flour and then you have a worker. You have those three things, but nothing happens until the worker goes to the machine with the flour and starts working. Then you have bread. Marx said that there is an input of labour value, and the employer uses that value to put a price on the bread, which includes profit, and thus a surplus is created. The moment workers work on the machine, they generate a surplus called surplus value. Surplus value is what the employer takes as profit. That is how capitalism works.

The reason Marx was so interested in this is because something happens as the worker works on the machine in the factory – a working class is created. I started my political life as a trade unionist in Cape Town, and we used to go to the factories and say to the workers: 'You are working here, and without you nothing happens. The machinery and timber are there but it is very quiet. Suddenly the machine comes to life, you go there and you make a chair. Suddenly there is a chair, which is much more valuable. So you guys are the ones who create the extra. But who takes the extra? The boss, and he takes it as profit. What you get is a wage. The worker gets the wage, the employer gets the surplus value/profit.' This is the beginning of class consciousness.

When we talk about prices, remember that when a commodity goes to Pick n Pay and management decides there is too much available, they lower the price to get rid of it. If you go to Pick n Pay, you will see that the price of vegetables and fruit goes up and down. This tells us about supply and demand, but it tells nothing of class or where the commodity was created. There is an exchange going on: the price goes up and down, but they don't tell you how a value is created in the system of capitalism. We have to go to Marx to understand the system of capitalism, because Marx – and before him Adam Smith – analysed the labour theory of value, which explains how profit is actually determined.

When I was talking to the trade union movement, I asked how this related to the trade unions. What does a trade union do? They negotiate within a particular sector for a higher wage. The employer says: 'I've got these costs – I've got to pay for the flour, for the machines, make profit and pay labour. You are asking too much because the price I charge for my bread is determined by Pick n Pay, etc.' So there is competition around negotiation, and that is what trade unions are about. Trade unions exist within the structure of capitalism. Capitalism relies on the exploitation of labour using machines. If there are no machines and no raw materials and no worker, there is no capitalism. In the trade union movement, you fight for a higher piece of surplus value. The unions say that surplus value in this company is much too high, their profits are so high and workers want a chunk of that surplus value and the employer says, 'Wait a minute, you've got x proportion.' This is a debate that takes place all the time.

There is only one thing we need to add here about price, and that is collusion. The South African economy is notable for monopolisation and cartels. The Competition Commission examines competition in the market. The reason why I chose bread as an example is because bread producers have recently been fined because the tribunal determined that they were colluding to fix the price of bread. The major producers held secret meetings and decided to increase the bread price regardless of the cost of production. They ignored the laws of supply and demand and what we call 'bourgeois economics', and decided to fix the price. After they had all agreed to this, they approached Pick n Pay and others and laid down the price of bread. This is illegal in South Africa, but it is done all the time. We have not done enough research and scientific work to examine how the collusion happens.

To conclude this section, we need to understand how value is created in the economy – who gets what shares, and why, and whether the price that emerges from those negotiations is subject to the laws of supply and demand, as our market economics claims. In a free market there will be no collusion, as every employer will negotiate for himself/herself. In practice, it does not work like that; there is collusion, there are agreements, and this is how the price is often determined in many industries.

The topic of this chapter is the politics of economics. I have spent some time on the economics, and would now like to draw out a few quick points about the politics of all this. Firstly, the discovery of classes within the capitalist system was a major idea because people like Marx began to analyse how classes were formed in capitalism, what motivated them and how they organised. They realised that under a developed capitalism there is a class of people that we call a capitalist class who own the means of production, like the factories. Below them is the working class, often called the proletariat. So, you have these two main classes. In modern society, you get the modern bourgeoisie, and the bourgeoisie is more than the capitalist class. We need to be very careful about this differentiation because the Strategy and Tactics document talks about the bourgeoisie and distinguishes different elements and strata of the bourgeoisie.

We ought to talk about the middle strata. Professional people who do not own factories, do not employ lots of workers and do not extract surplus value from their workers are said to occupy an 'in-between' position. The bourgeoisie includes the owners of the means of production, but also includes senior politicians, the rich, the elite, investors and people who own capital but not factories. Many of them do not actually work in a factory; it is not the old-style employer of labour. These are guys who play at the stock market, including some politicians who fall into that category. We call them the bourgeoisie, not the capitalist class. I tend to think we should distinguish between the two, but I do not want to get locked into semantic debates.

The next point I want to make is that within capitalism, a state emerges – the capitalist state. There is an excellent book on the capitalist state by the British Marxist academic Ralph Miliband. He wanted to clear up the confusion surrounding a clause in *The Communist Manifesto*, by Karl Marx and Friedrich Engels, stating that the capitalist class determines what the state does. There is a very strong link between the capitalist class and the state, but Miliband argues that in fact the state has a certain degree of relative autonomy. It is not totally independent/ autonomist, but it is relatively independent from the bourgeoisie, the capitalist class. Miliband stressed that we need to understand how the state works and what it does.

In conclusion, in my view we do not really understand what our state is and who determines what it does and why. In other words, who decides? If you want to tell me that Cabinet decides what our state does, remember that when Cabinet sits down and determines interest rates, or determines employment or economic policy, you can be quite sure that they discuss how business, the private sector and foreign investors will respond. The politics in which our Cabinet operates is very complicated. President Zuma, or any president, has to take account of many interests – foreign investors, local investors, local employers, local factory owners, local gamblers on the stock exchange and so on. When we talk about our state machinery, which is the Cabinet, when we pass a law we have to be careful. Every law we pass takes account of class interests – the interests of the bourgeoisie, of the working class, of the capitalist class. We do not just decide in a vacuum.

It is very important that we understand how the economy works, how things relate to each other, how employers relate to workers and what the role of the working class is in an economy – especially in industry, but also in the mines and in agriculture. Let us say a farmer has a good piece of land, as well as the seeds and the capital and a tractor. The only problem is labour. Until there is labour, nothing will happen. The tractor needs a driver, and the seeds will rot if no one plants them. Once the farmer acquires labour, he puts all of those factors to work and surplus value and commodities are created. Then the state comes and tells the farmer, you are making big profits and we are going to regulate your industry. You put your money into the banks, we want to know how much profit that bank is making; and the banks say, Steady on, if you regulate too much that farmer will stop producing goods.

These are complex issues that we refer to as the politics of economics, or political economy, and it is essential that we study and explore them in order to understand the country we live in.

Chapter 7

Race and Class

In this chapter I will address the issue of race and class. Under apartheid, the struggle was about the system of white minority rule and not only against racial discrimination. How has this changed under ANC rule? What social forces are at work?

The character of the national liberation struggle

In preparing for this session, I compared the 1969 Morogoro document on Strategy and Tactics with the 2007 Polokwane Strategy and Tactics. This inspired me to write a brief speculative piece entitled 'Thesis on the transition', which is intended to stimulate discussion. In it I make one crucial point: in 1969, the system was defined as internal colonialism or colonialism of a special type (CST). In political theory, colonialism is defined in a certain way: a colonial system is one in which a foreign power controls the state, the army and the administration, and imposes a certain ideology on the subject people. But when you look at the system now, after more than fifteen years of ANC rule, you find that many of those criteria or chief characteristics of classical colonialism no longer apply. We do not have a colonial state; the state is controlled by the ANC. We do not have a foreign judiciary or a foreign army. We do not have a foreign administration, and we do not have a foreign ideology of race inferiority in the schools. I may be wrong, but I would suggest that we really need a new formulation to explain the character of our current system.

When the ANC was formed, and indeed at Morogoro in

1969, the main objective was to identify the social forces which would fight for national liberation, and these social forces were defined in a system of internal colonialism. The liberation movement insisted that its task was national liberation, and this determined the character of the movement. We need to remember that at Morogoro, and since, there were individual members of the movement who kept raising class struggle and capitalism. But it was stated very clearly that while we understand the class nature of our system, the national character must be dominant. That was obviously the correct position at the time because the main driving force for change in South Africa has always been the African masses. They were the most oppressed and the largest component, and therefore their understanding of their environment and problems was national. While the system of race discrimination existed, it was more than race discrimination – it was actually a colonial system of white domination. Morogoro also stated that in the early years of the 20th century national consciousness among the African people grew strongly, and this national consciousness led to the formation of the ANC to unite the various tribes and articulate a policy of national emancipation.

But Morogoro also stated 'that nationalism must not be confused with chauvinism or narrow nationalism'. In recent years, some ANC members have been accused of espousing chauvinist and narrow nationalism. This is not a new issue. Morogoro deals with it, and if you read the Strategy and Tactics of 1969 you will see that this issue was dealt with in the ANC at that time. What the ANC says is that although it is, and was, a national liberation movement, this must not be confused with black chauvinism and/or narrow nationalism.

We can illustrate this point in relation to the emergence of black power in the United States in the mid-1960s. The civil rights leader Stokely Carmichael started a movement that was sharply anti-white and focused on black discrimination and black power. The ANC did not support this, and took a stand saying that this was not a progressive movement in the overall context because it was chauvinistic and narrowly nationalist. Similarly, when the Pan Africanist Congress (PAC) was formed, it was anti-communist, chauvinist and anti-white. People like Josias Madzunya pushed for a 'black power' kind of policy, and the ANC took a position against this. The ANC declared that the policy for South Africa was the Freedom Charter, which states that South Africa belongs to all who live in it, black and white. Even if you have a national movement of primarily African liberation, this does not mean that the vision is black power. So this issue of chauvinism and narrow nationalism was dealt with in 1969, and it is amazing to me that some people in our movement do not know this, or have forgotten it.

Another important sentence on this issue contained in the Morogoro Strategy and Tactics document states: 'the confrontation on the lines of colour is not of our choosing.' The ANC was very careful to say that the colour lines in South Africa were created by internal colonialism, not by the African people. A long time ago, the ANC was very careful to say: we are not chauvinistic, we are not narrow nationalist, and we have a vision of inclusiveness. We must be very clear about what the ANC is and is not. It certainly is not an anti-white movement and it never has been.

From the very beginning, ANC policy recognised that the African masses were the main force for liberation. However, the Morogoro document also dealt with the issue of other oppressed non-white groups, a question which is not dealt with much in the 2007 Polokwane Strategy and Tactics document. It is important to see why Morogoro dealt with this. The document acknowledged that there are other oppressed non-white groups in South Africa – 2 million Coloureds (in those days), and 750 000 Indian people who 'have suffered national humiliation, discrimination and oppression'. In terms of the actual practical aspects of the struggle, it was very important to get Coloured and Indian people into an alliance with the ANC. Since these people had also suffered various forms of humiliation, discrimination and oppression, the ANC said that they constituted an integral part of the social forces against white supremacy, even though the main content of the national liberation struggle was the liberation of the Africans in particular.

What of the role of whites? The Morogoro document recognised that a small group of revolutionary whites played an honourable role in the struggle, including in the Congress of Democrats and within Umkhonto weSizwe, and 'that white comrades must be fully integrated in the movement on the basis on individual equality'. This is why comrades like Yusuf Dadoo, Reggie September and Joe Slovo were incorporated into the ANC Revolutionary Council in 1969 on the basis of equality. People in the movement insisted that they should be treated equally, and that was very strongly stipulated. However, there was also an implicit understanding that the movement should be under African leadership. In the Congress Alliance we always said that the ANC president should be an African, and although this was not in writing, it has been the case to date – from Albert Luthuli and Oliver Tambo to the president of the ANC today.

As far as the white working class was concerned, the document stated that the white working class formed part of the ruling group but in the long run might come to see that their interests coincide those of non-white workers. It was hoped that in the future African, Coloured and Indian trade unions would persuade the white working class to participate in the struggle. With regard to the white population as a whole, the Morogoro document says that the white population has been embedded in the country for more than three centuries, and is thus an alien body only in the historical sense. The internal colonialism thesis argued that whites in South Africa were acting like a colonial power. This is significant because often some comrades forget that while whites may be discriminatory they are still South Africans.

With regard to the working class, the Morogoro document says that a working class struggle would embrace more than formal democracy, and thus the drive towards national emancipation is bound up with economic emancipation. When we talk about emancipation, we need to be clear about the nature of the South African economy. Certain documents have argued that the structure of the South African economy has not changed in over a century. The document from Polokwane states that the relations of production remain unchanged. In Strategy and Tactics it is stated that there will be no emancipation for workers unless we change the structure of the economy. What does Polokwane say about this? It says the national democratic revolution (NDR) seeks to eradicate the specific relations of production that underpinned super-exploitation but it does not eradicate capitalist relations of production. The ANC accepts that capitalist production is here, though not forever, and the object of the NDR is not to remove capitalist relations of production, but to remove the structures which created super-exploitation. One must be very clear on this issue. ANC policy is not against capitalism as such, certainly in the present era; it is against monopoly capital and super-exploitative relations of production. If you read the economic clauses of the Freedom Charter carefully, that is what is said.

At a recent Youth League meeting somebody got up and said the ANC does not like to talk about class. Fortunately I had the Polokwane document with me, and this is what it says: in class terms, the forces for liberation are black workers, the employed and unemployed, rural and urban workers, the middle strata, small business and real aspirant capitalists. In other words, the ANC is a middle-class movement embracing all those people and all those forces. Polokwane said something else interesting about the middle strata, and this is an important point. The black middle class is critical, including the intelligentsia, small business people and the black capitalist group which sees the revolution serving their interests, and that for me is problematic. I do not see signs that the black capitalist class in general agrees that the revolution we speak of here – the removal of super-exploitation – serves their interests. Instead, I see a degree of compradorisation by certain elements of the black capitalist class – but we can argue about that.

The Polokwane document also says that a section of the black capitalist class is susceptible to cooption and could develop into a comprador bourgeoisie. We really need more research into the black capitalist class to answer the questions: Who are compradors? Who has an interest in developing the national productive forces? Where are they going, and what is the scientific evidence on this process? We need far more research and analysis because the situation is rather vague.

Who is the enemy?

Now we come to the critical issue: who is the enemy? At Morogoro, the ANC defined the enemy as white minority rule. At Polokwane, the chief enemy of the NDR was defined as monopoly capital, but this has not been developed further. We do not do that kind of analysis in the ANC; I think we are too scared to. For example, in the Green Paper on Planning from the Presidency no enemy is identified. The Strategy and Tactics document from Polokwane identified an enemy – monopoly capital. It seems to me that whatever we say in government or in Parliament, we understand exactly who we are fighting and what the problem is. I am bothered about where we are going and what we should do, and many comrades are asking these questions. It's all very well to talk in Parliament about pulling the whole nation together, cooperating, and so on, but as the ANC we need to be more scientific. With that in mind, I will conclude this chapter with the following suggestions.

Firstly, since the structure of the economy remains unchanged, all the documents I have talked about say that we must recognise that small reforms and adjustments will not make that much difference because the structure is what underpins everything. So let's be careful about reforms. Secondly, we need to analyse the structure of the economy. What is its character? What is monopoly capital, what is its role and what does it do? Thirdly, there are fault lines in the economy. What are those fault lines and where do these fit in the overall structure of the economy? Once you recognise that there are certain fundamental cleavages in this country, which actually maintain the status quo, only then can we understand where incremental reforms fit into the overall structure. Unless we change the overall structure, we will be in the same situation forever.

In the days of Morogoro it was very clear who owned and controlled the economy. Today we need to identify these issues more clearly and see what remains of the colonial legacy in South Africa in structural terms, particularly with regard to the economy. In my view, while we recognise that traditionally the ANC was a liberation movement of the oppressed people, with African people being the dominant group and exercising leadership, we cannot maintain that formulation forever. In my view, it is our task today to reformulate rigorously where we are – not only in race or national terms, but also in class terms.

Finally, on the question of non-racialism, within the movement we were all comrades, of all colours. In society as a whole today, we have non-racialism (under African leadership) and the ANC is a non-racial movement. Within the movement we do not discriminate and we are all equal members of the ANC under an African president. But looking forward to the future, people are asking how we are building a non-racial future through this non-racial movement located in a society which is still highly segregated. This is going to be a non-racial society in which people of all colours are going to want a place, and the

Constitution guarantees them that place. It seems to me that we need to begin to discuss how to go forward into a future which is non-racial and accommodates all races equally and finally overcomes the whole colonial legacy.

Chapter 8
The Politics of Job Creation

Let me start with two statements. Firstly, politics has always played a major role in employment issues in South Africa. Secondly, even when our economy was moving and growing quite well in 2001/02 under the ANC government, we still had a very high unemployment rate of 22 per cent.

Why do I talk about the importance of politics in employment, and why do I say that even when our economy grew well we still had high unemployment? I do so because as the ANC we have to look at both those things.

Let's look at politics and unemployment. Firstly, the apartheid system was based on forced, cheap, migrant labour. That is what it was all about. Of course there was racial prejudice, but fundamentally the whole system was built on the mining industry and the use of migrant labour. I'm sure we all know that.

Secondly, the exploitation that came under apartheid was based on race, class and gender. That is why we used to talk about the triple oppression of women, although we do not seem to talk about it anymore. Now it is all gender, but the ANC policy was to combat the triple oppression of women by race, class and gender.

Thirdly, the ANC has said continually that the system of apartheid was a system of monopoly capitalism. If you read the papers these days, you can see that there is collusion between cartels to keep prices high and exploit labour. The papers are full of it. So monopoly capitalism is what the ANC talked about. Clearly, many of these things are still here now under an ANC government, and so we have to ask: is there a role for politics since we are the ruling party? What can we as a party do, politically, not economically only, to change the employment situation? It's a political question, I believe, and I think the ANC believes it.

Let me turn to the question of unemployment. Even when the economy was growing well, we still had 22 per cent unemployment. The economy is not growing much now; it was growing better in 2001/02, yet we still had chronic unemployment. Why? The answer is that unemployment is structural. Apartheid gave us a system in which unemployment was structural. If the Minister of Public Works is going to increase the scope of the Expanded Public Works Programme, is that going to tackle the structure that we inherited? Is it going to get rid of the 22 per cent unemployment, which is now 28 per cent and even 40 per cent if you calculate it differently? Are we talking about the right things? When we say we're going to increase social grants or expand public works or talk to the state-owned enterprises and say they must increase employment, or when the DTI says we are going to move to labour-intensive manufacturing, is that going to get rid of the 22 per cent? What is the politics of all this? It seems to me that the key to what we are talking about is to restructure the way the economy grows by restructuring the growth path. The Presidency talks about an inclusive growth path, while Ebrahim Patel proposes a developmental growth path, and so on. Many different versions of growth are on the table.

Will this kind of analysis get rid of the 22 per cent? If you read Trevor Manuel's Green Paper on National Strategic Planning (September 2009), you will see that it says that the structure of the economy has not changed for a hundred years. Frankly, many of our current documents say we have not changed the structure of the economy. What do we do? Clearly, changing the structure of the economy is not just an economic matter. You cannot go to the Minister of Trade and Industry or the Minister of Public Enterprises and tell them to change the structure of the economy. This is a political matter, and decisions will need to be taken about the fundamentals of the economy we inherited from apartheid. We are not going to be able to handle it piecemeal, making adjustments here and there.

Who is going to do this? The private sector? Well, why should the private sector change the structure of the economy? They benefit very well; our businesspeople are doing much better than they have ever done. Inequality in South Africa is higher than in 1994. What that means is that the rich are richer than they were because the poor are not that much richer than they were. Something has happened. Why should private business change the structure of the economy? Yes, you can say to them you must train some people, you must have apprenticeship, skills training and all that, but that also won't change the structure of the economy. Why should they do it? Because their profits depend on the inherited structure, cheap labour and a pool of millions of unemployed people. This is what the labour brokers are doing. They take one group of people and they replace them with another group of people who just switch around and get lower pay. You ask any textile or garment factory in Cape Town and they will tell you that when a worker rises to a certain level of wages, that worker is fired and you get a young 16-year-old girl out of school, at the bottom wage, to replace that person – this is recycled labour. Why should the employer change the structure he inherited?

Let's take the ownership of the mining sector: the mines are still owned largely by the people who owned them before. Take manufacturing: the big factories are still owned by the people who owned them before. Yes, there is a bit of black empowerment, black faces fronting and all that, and we know all about it. If you fly South African Airways and you look at who is in business class, you will see that not much has changed. The ownership of manufacturing, of mining fundamentally, the people who count, has not changed a great deal. And in agriculture it's the same.

Are these the people who are going to restructure the economy?

Some comrades are saying we must push them to create jobs, push them by incentives and so on. Yes, we can do something there, and some comrades are saying the services sector (like insurance) will create a lot of jobs. That is true, but will increasing the number of people in the services sector change the overall structure of the economy?

How do we deal with the monopolies? We have allowed monopolies to concentrate. The Competition Commission of the DTI has done a lot of work on monopolies. South Africa is full of monopolies. Many of them are foreign-owned, and many take their profits overseas. Take Anglo American, for instance: 30 years ago Anglo American sent their design studios, which were in Main Street, Johannesburg where they had fantastic engineering designers, and they relocated them all to London. Then Anglo American listed on the London Stock Exchange, followed by Old Mutual. The big corporations are not South African anymore; they are listed in London, under foreign ownership. We say we want to change the system, but these things belong to them.

How do we deal with this? How do we push for job creation? The private sector is not going to do it for us. Can we create jobs through the public sector? Then there is national, provincial and local government – can we create jobs there?

When Julius Nyerere came into power in Tanzania, he said that for every nine public servants, the government should employ one more. Just increase the public service by 10 per cent. It did soak up a lot of unemployment. Of course, it led to certain inefficiencies, and there are problems with doing that. When I was in Cuba, I saw a group of six workers who were cutting the grass in a square. Two were cutting the grass and the other four were watching them. One has to be very careful, but nevertheless the private sector won't do anything. We have to do it.

We've allowed the state-owned enterprises to become a law unto themselves. In the committees that I've been on, for years we've asked the state-owned enterprises what motivates them. They would always come along and say their profit is such and such. Even when the IDC come here the first thing they say is, we've had a very good year, we've made a big profit. Who asked them to make a profit? They've got a job to do to build the economy; they are our private sector. This is where the political will comes in. We, as the ANC, have to tell them that their job is not to make a profit but to build the economy. We don't want them to lose, and we don't want to subsidise them, but we don't want them to have a capitalist mentality and we don't want them to pay capitalist bonuses and shares. Let the private sector do that – and even they should not do it.

Then take the development finance institutions (DFIs), like the Development Bank of Southern Africa (DBSA). When I came back from exile I was invited by the then chief executive to meet the bank's researchers and policy-makers. There were a lot of them doing research and developing policy, but when we adopted certain policies they were told the bank must make a profit or be closed down. That is why today the DBSA is basically a commercial bank, lending money to municipalities to make a profit or a return.

Let me leave the public sector and turn to the question of rural or urban development. In some of our committees comrades keep raising the question of rural development, and I am afraid to say that until Polokwane we did very little about it. The Polokwane Resolution on Rural Development is excellent. The question is, can we make jobs in the rural areas? If we do not make jobs there, the people are all going to come to the cities – and they're doing so anyway. All of our cities are flooded with people from the rural areas. Do we want that? Do we want more informal settlements all over South Africa? Can't we, as the ANC, not as government, say we want a policy to create jobs in the rural areas and the state must do it? The private sector will not do it. The private sector is not interested in going into the rural areas, so the state must do it. So, we need both rural and urban development, and the rural issue is important.

I want to touch on the question of decent work. COSATU has been pushing very hard for the ANC to adopt the policy of decent work. The question often arises: what do you mean by decent work? Do you mean good factory jobs at high pay or good government jobs at high pay? What if somebody is in a rural area, far from any factory, and he is not going to get a job in government, what does the ANC offer those people? Decent work? What about somebody in a squatter camp in Cape Town or Johannesburg, for example, who has no skills and who has no education and who is not going to get a job in a factory or in government? What does the ANC policy of decent work mean for that person? I am saying that there is no easy answer. What does it mean to somebody who is a car cleaner? What does it mean for some woman who is selling oranges on the street to earn a living? What about part-time workers or voluntary workers or women who do unpaid work like fetching water and firewood? What does the policy of decent work mean for them?

It is a good policy, but the ANC must be very clever in the way we convey this to the people; otherwise, many unemployed, self-employed and casual workers are going to say that the ANC is only working for factory workers and government employees, namely the formal sector. If you go to a squatter camp and talk about decent work, people are just going to laugh. They call it 'slogans'. We need policies that are real and which affect the poorest of the poor, including unpaid labour and women's unpaid work. How does decent work fit in there?

There are many challenges around creating jobs. It is not a mechanical thing. This is a political question, and we need to ask if we, as the ANC and as parliamentarians, are thinking politically about the economy we inherited, about structural unemployment. Are we going to try and transform this? Capitalism is not going to do it.

Chapter 9

After the Political Kingdom: The Economic Challenge Facing the ANC

'The structure of our economy has not changed significantly in a hundred years, it is still dominated by extractive and related industries.'
– Green Paper: National Strategic Planning, 2009, p. 7

'Colonial relations in some centres of power, especially the economy, remain largely unchanged.'
– Strategy and Tactics, 2009, p. 14

The foundations of apartheid oppression were both political and economic. The left argued that the economic structure would have to change if political and social reforms were to be effective. However, as the negotiated settlement came into view, the focus was on removing the apartheid state from power, and an 'understanding' was reached with capital that no radical attack was intended. Furthermore, the IMF and World Bank exerted pressure on the ANC not to interfere with market capitalism and to observe conservative fiscal and monetary policies. As the ANC came to power, it adopted reformist policies designed to relieve the inhuman conditions of the masses. Economic policy focused on deracialising the economy and empowering black people.

The powerful role of capital over the economy, as owners

and controllers, was downplayed except insofar as it was discriminatory. There were various tentative proposals for a partnership between the state and capital. However, the economy has stalled, inequality has increased, and massive social problems remain. Is this a case of market failure typical of post-colonial capitalism in Africa? Since the ANC government has little power over the critical economic decisions taken by capital, the question arises whether the role of capital should be reopened, particularly as there is a growing concern that the inherited structure of the economy is a block to further progress in both social and economic areas. A direct assault on capital – for example, through nationalisation – may not be feasible, but the only alternative seems to be a substantial increase in the role of the state, not only in its regulatory powers but also in its power to direct capital to invest in productive activity in the real economy. Is the ANC government willing to take this on?

Africa's post-colonial experience

The anti-colonial struggle across Africa has generally placed political freedom in the forefront, as was illustrated by Kwame Nkrumah's call: 'Seek ye first the political kingdom and all else will come unto ye.' Social rights was a close second, and African governments moved swiftly to improve health and education provision, among other important social services. Economic issues have generally been treated more ambiguously. Only after Ghana's government had been in power for some years did Nkrumah tackle the economy directly. Julius Nyerere and Kenneth Kaunda began nationalisation some years after taking political power, although their efforts proved to be less successful than the postwar European nationalisations they sought to emulate.

In South Africa, the ANC was most emphatic about political and social rights, leaving economic rights to issues which might be called social democratic. The economic clause of the Freedom

Charter caused much difficulty to the leadership of the ANC, and was only accepted after assurances that the clauses would not lead to 'Communism'.

Now that the ANC has been in political power for over fifteen years, the challenge of economic policy has come to the fore, as it has become clear that the advances in political and social rights have limited effects as long as economic power remains outside its reach.

This paper will therefore address three questions:

1. How far along is the ANC in its historical mission of liberating the oppressed people of South Africa?
2. How far is the ANC government on the road to transforming the inherited economic structure as part of that mission?
3. What is the link between reform and economic transformation in the vision of the ANC?

The political transition in South Africa

The ANC has long held to the objective of the national democratic revolution (NDR). Since it has now been in government for 16 years, it is appropriate to ask to what extent the ANC has achieved this objective in whole or in part.

This paper will discuss this question first from a theoretical perspective, then by an analysis of ANC policy pronouncements over the years, and finally by an examination of the economy. The argument will be that while much has been achieved at the political level and some important reforms have been made at the social level, the failure to transform the economy means that the NDR must stall.

The ANC characterises the 1994 transition in rather modest terms as 'a democratic breakthrough'. But the ANC political victory has allowed it to achieve political power and to make substantial advances in the social realm. It is undeniable that the ANC has captured control of the state in all its dimensions, Parliament, the executive, provincial and local government, the public service, the parastatals, the security forces and many other sectors of the state system. Yet it cannot be said that this power in the state system has signalled the emergence of a new ruling class. At best there is now a governing class or state elite, though neither category really suits.

Ralph Miliband (1969:23) argued that 'In the Marxist scheme, the ruling class of capitalist society is that class which owns and controls the means of production and which is able, by virtue of the economic power thus conferred upon it, to use the state as its instrument for the domination of society'. He quotes Marx as saying, 'The executive of the modern state is but a committee for managing the common affairs of the whole bourgeoisie,' and the state was above all the coercive instrument of a ruling class, itself defined in terms of its ownership and control of the means of production (Miliband, 1969:7).

Can this formulation be applied to post-apartheid South Africa? If so, what is the ruling class in South Africa, and is the ANC government serving its interests? Or is the ANC government serving the interests of its constituency, the broad multiclass mass of black people? Because of the dominance of the ANC in the state system, these questions are not easy to answer, even if the economically dominant class – business – is doing very well under ANC rule.

Miliband (1969:51) clarified many aspects of the relation between the state and economic power. He argued that in the capitalist system 'the capitalist class does not actually govern' and it is 'the state elite which does wield state power, as a distinct and separate entity'. The state has a degree of relative autonomy but nevertheless ensures that capitalist interests are protected, especially by using its coercive power to discipline the workers and the masses generally.

Furthermore, concentrated capitalist power provides a massive preponderance in society, which is exercised through 'political socialisation' by many other institutions outside the state system. A government or a ruling class has to exercise hegemony through the influence of institutions such as the education system, the religious institutions, the media and many other arenas where public opinion is generated and is broadly supportive of the inherited social values of market capitalism. As Marx put it, 'the ideas of the ruling class are in every epoch the ruling ideas' (Miliband, 1969:162).

So what is the relationship in South Africa between the economically dominant class and the state? Clearly this class has a great deal of influence over national economic decisions, but is its influence decisive, despite it not being the governing class? There is an important difference between the personnel who manage the state system in developed capitalist countries, who are largely drawn from the top layers of society (even where labour or social democratic parties are in office), and those who manage the South African state, who are drawn from the struggle ranks of the ANC. Can our state elite avoid the trap created in advanced capitalist countries where 'social-democratic leaders have eagerly bent themselves to the administration of the capitalist state, thereby strengthening the capitalist state' (Miliband, 1969:244)?

The ANC in the modern period characterised apartheid as 'a system of capitalist exploitation based on colonial racial relations'. During the period of negotiations, it began to argue that 'While the system of super-exploitation of the black majority all along fully served the interests of big business and the state, this has become a brake on the development of the economy as a whole' (ANC, 1991:4). This formulation suggests that business may be willing to assist in overcoming the apartheid system as a matter of self-interest.

Understandably, faced with the intransigence of the apartheid state, the ANC was willing to show that it would act 'responsibly' in economic matters, in the event of its accession to state power. Having stated that 'the vast bulk of productive assets are concentrated in the hands of a small number of conglomerates', it argues that 'growth in a democratic South Africa must be oriented towards satisfying the basic needs of the majority and empowering those who are disadvantaged and deprived.' The solution lies in 'a progressive redistribution of resources to the poor'. However, 'Redistribution needs also to take place within a framework of responsible fiscal and monetary discipline' (Draft Resolution on ANC Economic Policy, Department of Economic Policy, 11 May 1991). This formula was slipped into the RDP at the last stages and has since become a mantra in all statements on the economy.

The caution with respect to how the economy would be handled, and how capital itself would fare in the new democratic state, was also justified by the distinction between a 'democratic' and a 'socialist' agenda. In the 'democratic' phase, capital, even apartheid capital, could coexist with a democratic government without hindrance.

Thabo Mbeki set out the distinction between the democratic stage and the socialist stage in *New Agenda* (Mbeki, 2007:5): 'There is a distinct, material and historically determined difference between the national democratic and the socialist revolutions. The ANC accepted the proposition that our ally, the SACP, and not the ANC, would lead the forces and the struggle for the victory of the socialist revolution … Our movement has never stopped or discouraged the SACP from playing this role, and will not do so today or tomorrow. The objective reality in our country is that the victory of the socialist revolution cannot be achieved outside the context of the victory of the NDR.'

Mbeki then refers to a document where the character of the democratic revolution was set out ('The State and Social Transformation', an ANC discussion document dated January 1997). The document opened with the call for 'social and economic transformation of South African society. This objective had to be achieved in conditions where there had been a 'partnership between successive white minority governments and the capitalist class ... which practised "maximising the super-exploitation of the oppressed majority". It was because of the combination of political and economic oppression that 'the national liberation movement has, over 70 years, contained within itself both a nationalist and socialist tendency' (ANC, 1997a:10).

The document proceeds to discuss 'the graduated creation of a democratic state to replace the apartheid state' and to set out the relationship between the democratic state and owners of private capital based on 'mutual benefit'. This is to 'ensure that the state and capital act in concert'; the intention is to establish 'a dialectical relationship with private capital as a social partner for development and social progress' in order to ensure 'the mobilisation of the surplus both domestically and internationally'. The days of the 'robber barons' are clearly over.

The document goes on to discuss 'the deracialisation and democratisation of the economy', which should not be understood as 'black economic empowerment whose only and ultimate goal is only the creation of a "black bourgeoisie"' (ANC, 1997a:25). 'The democratic state has an objective interest in ensuring that a "black bourgeoisie" does not get formed as a result of theft of public resources, or the prostitution of particular nationals by foreign capital' (ANC, 1997a:27) as this would be 'fatal' for democracy.

This document brought a response in the shape of 'The State, Property Relations and Social Transformation', an unsigned document of 1998 drafted as 'A discussion paper towards the Alliance Summit' and published in *Umrabulo* No. 5 (1998). Although careful not to dissociate itself from the previous document, it goes much further in transforming the state, and does not comment directly on the proposal for a partnership between the state and capital, which is a wholly new proposition within the liberation movement.

These contrasting views of the relation of the new democratic state with capital reflect two strands in the liberation movement, previously referred to as the nationalist and the socialist strand. But what are we to make of the proposition that the state and capital should be 'social partners'? Does it suggest some kind of alliance, or is it only an understanding that the new state could work with capital for limited common goals?

As we have seen, some understanding was arrived at with big business in the external consultations prior to the negotiated settlement that the ANC would not take a hostile stance against capital even though the latter had been a 'partner' in apartheid oppression. The main focus at the time was on removing the apartheid grip on the state; business could be dealt with subsequently. This stance was reinforced by the enormous pressures from the IMF and World Bank for the ANC to present a 'responsible' economic posture, including the promotion of fiscal and monetary discipline as an essential part of economic policy. Nevertheless, none of the versions of Strategy and Tactics refers to a 'partnership' between the state and capital, even if there is an explicit reference to an acceptance that the democratic state would not resolve the contradictions between capital and labour.

ANC economic policy

While the political agenda has been clear, the economic agenda has been far less so. Arguably, the most obvious achievements have been in the area of BEE and in the extension of social welfare and social services, which has certainly made an difference in humanising what remains a severely unequal system. For the rest, while there are numerous policy documents and statements, with far-reaching propositions, it is difficult to pin down actual policy on transformation of the inherited structure.

We may identify some key moments of economic policy formation, notably Morogoro in 1969, Kabwe in 1985, Durban in

1991 and Polokwane in 2007. Let us begin this quick survey with a quote from the National Conference at Polokwane. Having posited a 'mixed economy, where state, cooperative and other forms of social ownership exist together with private capital in a constructive relationship …', the document goes on to state: 'The symbiosis between political oppression and the apartheid capitalist system was so strong that, *if decisive action is not taken to deal with economic subjugation and exclusion, the essence of apartheid will remain* [my emphasis], with a few black men and women incorporated into the courtyard of privilege. The old fault lines will persist and social stability will be threatened. Without a fundamental transformation of economic relations the very democracy for which so many sacrificed could be placed in jeopardy' (ANC, 2007b:3–4).

So what is this 'fundamental transformation of economic relations'?

At Mafikeng in 1997, the National Congress of the ANC resolved 'that the mission of the ANC continues to be the fundamental transformation of the South African economy'. This is in order to 'empower black people, especially Africans, eliminate poverty and the extreme inequalities generated by the apartheid system'. The Resolution on Economic Transformation from Mafikeng makes no reference to the relationship with capital, but there is a substantial section dealing with macroeconomic policy and a range of reforms in industrial and trade policy, among others.

The challenge of transforming the inherited economic structure

The economic history of South Africa can largely be told in terms of the dominance of a few large conglomerates, controlled by families through pyramid structures (Black & Roberts, in Aron, 2009:216). 'The economy remains highly concentrated. The five conglomerate groupings led by Anglo American still controlled

44.6 per cent of the capitalisation of the JSE in 2006, though this was well down from 83.8 per cent in 1990 (Black & Roberts, in Aron, 2009:227).

The apartheid state industrialised through strong industrial policy interventions, particularly in mining, energy and resource-processing industries. Hence the real economy is well linked to capital- and electricity-intensive mining and mineral-processing activities, which in turn account for the bulk of exports (ETC, n.d.:1). 'The dominant firms have often attained pre-eminence in part through the legacy of state support and protection for heavy industry' (Black & Roberts, in Aron, 2009:227). The state enterprises continue to supply electricity to large and energy-intensive industries at significantly lower prices than for other industries (Black & Roberts, in Aron, 2009:237).

By the mid-2000s, South Africa was still a classic mining-based economy. After 1994, the rapid growth of resource-based and capital-intensive industries far outstripped manufacturing. 'Exports remain dominated by minerals and resource-intensive manufactured products. Minerals etc. remain about 60 per cent of total merchandise exports' (Black & Roberts, in Aron, 2009:221). As for other exports, 'a significant portion of exports is due to re-export of imported products by SA distributors to southern African markets' (Black & Roberts, in Aron, 2009:222).

Although mining contributed about 10 per cent of GDP and employment, it still accounted for half of exports. Thus the country is uncomfortably dependent on international commodity prices. So state revenues are uneven, the benefits are also confined to a small group and inequalities remain large. The mines are islands in the economy and there is little downstream benefit.

The growth path remains fragile, dependent on excessive consumer credit, elite consumer spending, and portfolio flows. We remain captive to the 'far-reaching exertion of market power by large firms, unilaterally and in oligopolies through coordinated behaviour' (Black & Roberts, in Aron, 2009:239).

Table 1: Contributions to GDP

	2006
Manufacturing	18.0%
Electricity, gas, water	2.4%
Construction	3.3%
Trade etc	15.4%
Transport etc	10.8%
Financial and business services	21.6%
Other services	5.9%
Government	13.9%
Agriculture	2.4 %
Mining	6.4%

(*Source: The SA Economy, IDC, 14 March 2007*)

We seem to have followed the economic models of the advanced economies, which have seen major bubbles, with disastrous consequences. A glaring issue in South Africa is the excessive financialisation in the economy, which is not financing investment in productive activity.

Structural financial imbalances

The high deficit on the current account is dependent on foreign financial inflows, which are mainly 'hot' money rather than foreign direct investment (FDI). Dividend and interest payments to foreigners with capital outflows for 2007/08 were about 3.5 per cent of GDP. The final judgment on the financial performance must be in terms of comparisons with other middle-income countries – for example, Hungary, Poland, Turkey, Brazil, Chile and Malaysia – as summarised in Table 2.

The deficit of almost 10 per cent of GDP on the current account is attributed to the following: balance of trade, including gold (1.5 per cent), net service payments (4 per cent), net income payments (3.5 per cent), current transfers (1 per cent).

Table 2: Comparative financial performance

Income per capita	SA $10,880	Others $7,252
Growth GDP 1994–2005	3.3%	4.6%
GFCF	15.9%	24.6%
Industrial value added per GDP	26.9%	37.1%
Growth in exports	4.6 %	9.4 %
Total exports per GDP 2005	27.1%	37.9%

(*Source: Black & Roberts, in Aron, 2009:213*)

The structure of value chains

The weight of support has continued to focus on larger-scale capital-intensive activities (Black & Roberts, in Aron, 2009:215). 'The combination of liberalisation and incentives failed to achieve the improved export performance sought' (Black & Roberts, in Aron, 2009:224). We have not managed beneficiation well; for example, one third of the pulp produced in South Africa is processed elsewhere (Black & Roberts, in Aron, 2009:225).

Many DTI documents have discussed improving the value chain of production. Some now argue that the most viable value chains to create employment are agriculture, light industry, construction and services. We need a thorough discussion on the role of medium and heavy industry in South Africa's future economic advance.

Social effects

Because of the skewed economy, unemployment, poverty and inequality remain very high by world standards. Inequality remains at 1994 levels. There is an inequitable distribution of income, assets (and consequently wealth) and opportunities. This is perhaps the worst aspect of ANC rule.

The data on employment (see Table 3) is often interpreted in different ways, giving different percentages.

Table 3: Selected unemployment data

	1995	2003
Labour force (narrow)	11.6 m	16.1m (note large growth in labour force)
Labour force (broad)	13.6m	19.9m (NB: 'broad' includes discouraged workers)
Wage employment	8.2 m	9.5m
Self-employed	1.4 m	2.1m
Unemployed (narrow)	1.9 m	4.5m
Unemployed (broad)	4.0m	8.3m
Unemployment rate (narrow)	17	28
Unemployment rate (broad)	29	42

(*Source: Kingdon & Knight, in Aron, 2009:300*)

The absorption rate, which in many ways is a better indicator than the unemployment rate, and which reflects the number of working adults who say they are employed, stood at 48 per cent (narrow), 56 per cent (broad) in 1995, but improved to 54 per cent (narrow) and 67 per cent (broad) by 2003 (Kingdon & Knight, in Aron, 2009:303). The employment statistics are bedevilled by the large flow of new entrants into the labour pool, so percentages distort the situation. Most job creation since 2000 has been in construction, retail and services (public and private). In general, government policies have not led to job creation.

Also, taking the economy as a whole, there has been a substantial increase in the working poor, particularly in the informal sector, which had 34 per cent of the 2003 labour force (Kingdon & Knight, in Aron, 2009:309). Real earnings of wage employees fell only slowly, by 1.6 per cent between 1995 and 2003 (Kingdon & Knight, in Aron, 2009:307). According to Kingdon, 'there is a general consensus that poverty rose over the post-apartheid period' (Kingdon & Knight, in Aron, 2009:322), but this finding is not actually agreed by all researchers.

Once again, GEAR

Was GEAR an attempt at curbing a downward spiral or dealing with the structural legacy of apartheid? Most would say it was the former. GEAR brought a decisive shift in fiscal policy, reversing the increase in government spending begun in 1994. The most critical aspect was the decline in spending on infrastructure (mostly capital). At the same time, it introduced trade liberalisation and international competitiveness as costly central objectives, as well as some privatisation of state-owned enterprises.

While spending on social services, health, education, welfare, police and prisons remained steady, the effect was that spending per capita fell due to population growth of about 7 per cent. Indeed, most government statistics omit the effect of population growth and often refer to nominal rather than real spending, thereby concealing the actual spending impact.

But growth rates after the adoption of GEAR in 1996 fell from 4.2 per cent to 1 per cent in 1998, rising again to 4.2 per cent in 2000. Thereafter, growth fluctuated between 3 and 5.5 per cent until 2007, when the economy crashed. In the years following, one in ten workers in the formal sector (excluding agriculture) lost their jobs, with the biggest losses in mining, construction and transport, key sectors for a growing economy. 'Particularly large job losses in absolute terms were in sectors which underwent major restructuring, partly as a result of import liberalisation' (Black & Roberts, in Aron, 2009:218).

In sum, GEAR reached some of its targets, such as the fiscal deficit, real government consumption and some reduction in inflation. However it failed to reach its targets in interest rates, private sector investment, GDP growth or employment. This means that the cost of reducing the deficit and tariff reductions was entirely disproportionate to the social outcomes, particularly job losses in manufacturing of over 100 000.

Financialisation of the economy

The global financial crisis has done a great deal to uncover the essential character of global capitalism. The operation of hedge funds and derivatives, among other instruments, has illustrated the extent of financialisation of economies across the globe based on low-equity investments and highly geared bank debt. These high-risk investments, now called 'toxic debt', have been unsustainable.

While South Africa seems to have exercised some control over this process, the effects of financialisation and international financial integration are also evident here.

However, this does not absolve our government from exercising its regulatory function over debt management by capital, albeit in a judicious manner. And this may have to go beyond the normal functions of the South African Reserve Bank and the Financial Services Board (FSB). To do so, we have to know not only who owns what, but also who manages and takes actual decisions – two very different functions.

The ownership issue has been dealt with in detail in Robin McGregor's *Who Owns Whom*. Some useful information has also been provided in the *Sunday Times* listings of income and wealth. But it is clear that, in many cases, ownership and wealth have little correlation with actual decision-making. In contemporary capitalism, decisions on investment are far too complicated for most owners of capital. Decisions are left to professionals, who are thereby enabled to cream off huge share benefits and bonuses. These benefits then become major incentives to engage in high-value, short-term investments in highly speculative deals. This feeds the spiral of financialisation, with the results that we have seen.

In South Africa, we have a particular public interest in examining these matters because of the inherited concentration of economic power. If the economy is to be transformed, we have to understand the actual levers of financial and economic decision-making, and not only ownership.

Institutions of control
The managers of investment funds exercise enormous influence on the flow of capital across the economy. The largest funds are public companies and are listed on the stock exchange. Generally the most influential person is the chairperson of the board, who is often the executive chairperson.

Private companies are not listed on the stock exchange, and are generally led by persons representing the major shareholders. Then there are the commercial banks. These are few in number, and leadership is provided by both the chairperson of the board and the CEO.

Also important in decision-making is a cluster of institutions composed of experts. These are grouped in trade and industry institutions (by sector), and include senior economists based in all the institutions listed above, accounting firms and legal firms.

Addressing the inherited structure
The purpose of this research is to investigate whether it is possible for the state to intervene to overcome the rigidities in the economy, to lessen the degree of concentration throughout the economy, and thereby to tackle the obstacles to creating a fairer and more democratic economy in which 'the people shall share in the country's wealth'. There are signs that even relatively conservative personalities and experts in business are beginning to recognise that a degree of government leadership over the economy is necessary, and they may be persuaded to participate in such a process even if it does not serve their immediate business interests. After all, that was the hallmark of the rapid growth of countries like South Korea. In any case, failure to plan the economy's transformation will surely lead to demands for

ever more radical action than what is proposed here.

This project has become necessary because it is now clear that adjustments to the social wage, by way of housing, improved access to health and education and social grants, are insufficient to overcome the social legacy of apartheid. Unemployment, poverty and inequality are too deeply embedded in the economic foundations of the system for them to be remedied by incremental means alone. This is now being increasingly recognised in our society, and even conservative interests in business now accept that we require major changes.

However, important policy-makers in government are not clear about what instruments are available within the present capitalist system to make significant change. The debate about nationalisation or socialisation is a sign of this difficulty.

It is the objective of this study to create an informed basis for such discussions so that practical and realistic answers can be found about the changes needed.

We shall make slow progress unless we address the concentration of economic power. This includes tackling the profits made by the large corporations. 'Altering the industrial development trajectory will need concerted action across public institutions' (Black & Roberts, in Aron, 2009:227). Black and Roberts argue that 'the main question is not ownership as such, but the changes to the conditions that underpin conduct and performance' (Black & Roberts, in Aron, 2009:233).

Are prescribed assets wholly out of question? Can we not be bolder in mobilising the vast financial assets in the country, and held abroad by our citizens, and deploy them for expanding our economy in a way that provides employment, has a multiplier effect in the economy and not only enhances the social wage, important as that is?

The state has a variety of financial and non-financial instruments which it can use to leverage change. These include the development finance institutions (DFIs), such as the

IDC, DBSA, NEF and Land Bank, state-owned enterprises – particularly Eskom and Transnet – as well as the Public Investment Corporation (PIC) and many regulatory mechanisms.

We have been shy of addressing the huge wealth of the rich. Income inequalities, high as they are, do not reflect the even larger inequalities of wealth, which indicate the massive assets of the rich – multiple properties, houses, land, cars, airplanes, etc. Should we not have a stronger wealth tax?

Creating a new base in the domestic economy

It is common cause that demand is too restricted and the productive base too small. Many similar economies, notably the Asian Tigers, had similar conditions and overcame them to become major industrial powers. South Korea curbed luxury imports and enforced domestic procurement, even insisting that foreign multinational corporations prove that local components were not available before allowing imports. Furthermore, many of these countries, including China, moved from last-stage assembly production, without research and development capacities, to fully self-reliant and self-sustaining capabilities in industrialisation with the aid of massive infant-industry protection. How can we diversify the South African economy away from minerals?

Classical political economy argues that a country must build its own means of production capability in order to grow, and this means factories which produce the basic elements of manufacturing. Is it the case that the modern global integrated and interdependent economic system has removed this basic requirement? Can a strong financial and service sector become the basic engine of growing the economy?

Mobilising political energy

Whenever public concerns rise about the performance of the economy, and labour in particular gets restless, there is either a Presidential Summit, or NEDLAC is brought in to articulate these concerns. Militant resolutions are also passed at meetings of COSATU and the SACP. ANC conference resolutions are more muted, but often also pose fundamental questions about economic policy. Yet change is slow and hesitant. Such efforts do not challenge the fundamental faults in the economy, nor seemingly do they challenge the huge inequalities of wealth and power in our society, which are clearly set out in documents like Strategy and Tactics (2009).

Nor are we making strenuous efforts to ensure popular participation in government. Instead we get popular protest action in many areas. What is wrong?

There is consensus on the need for a developmental state. On the analysis above, we are very far from that goal. Can we create new energy for a transformation agenda setting out stages for critical change?

Sources

Aron, Janine, Brian Kahn & Geeta Kingdon (2009). *South African economic policy under democracy*. Oxford: Oxford University Press.

Black, Anthony & Simon Roberts (2009). 'The evolution of industrial and competition policies, in Aron et al., 2009, *South African economic policy under democracy*. Oxford: Oxford University Press.

Kingdom, Geeta & John Knight (2009). 'Unemployment, South Africa's Achilles' Heel', in Aron et al., 2009, *South African economic policy under democracy*. Oxford: Oxford University Press.

Marx, Karl (1974). *Capital*. Volume 1. London: Lawrence & Wishart.

Miliband, Ralph (1969). *The State in Capitalist Society*. London: Quartet Books

Additional sources

I have also made extensive use of ideas and data from the following papers, without indicating the full source details as these are working drafts.

ANC (2007a). Economic transformation for a national democratic society. Discussion document for ANC Policy Conference, June 2007.

ANC (2007b). 52nd National Conference 2007, Policy Discussion Documents, *Umrabulo* Vol. 2.

ANC (2005). The Accelerated and Shared Growth Initiative for South Africa, Economic Transformation Committee, Johannesburg, 5 December 2005.

ANC (2003). Growth and Development Summit Agreement, 7 June 2003.

ANC (2002). Economic Transformation Committee Policy Conference, 21–23 June 2002.

ANC (2001a). A Growth, Development and Employment Accord for South Africa, ETC, Johannesburg, 20 July 2001.

ANC (2001b). Towards an Accelerated Growth Path. 4th draft discussion document, 20 July 2001.

ANC (2001). Special ETC Lekhotla, Johannesburg, 27 October 2001.

ANC (2000a). Declaration of the ANC National General Council, Port Elizabeth, 12–15 July 2000.

ANC (2000b). Draft Reports of the Commissions on Programme of Action, National General Council, 2000.

ANC (2000). Report Back from the ANC National General Council, 11–15 July 2000.

ANC (1998a). Working notes for ETC meeting, 8 May 1998.

ANC (1998b). *Umrabulo*, No. 5.

ANC (1997a). 'The state and social transformation'. ANC discussion document, January 1997.

ANC (1997b). Resolutions on economic transformation, Mafikeng Conference.

ANC (1991). Advance to National Democracy. Guidelines on Strategy and Tactics of the ANC, February 1991.

COSATU (undated). 'Overview of the economy'.

COSATU (undated). 'Labour input of the jobs crisis'.

Declaration of the Presidential Jobs Summit. Summary (undated).

ETC Task Team, (undated). 'Taking forward industrial policy in a South African developmental state'.

Makhetla, Neva (2009). 'A growth path for decent work'.

Makhetla, Neva (2009). 'Toward a more inclusive economy'. Conference on Government Policy and the Decent Work Agenda, May 2009.

Makhetla, Neva (2009). 'The international economic crisis and South Africa, in *New Agenda* (forthcoming).

Mbeki, Thabo (2007). Address to opening session of the ANC Policy Conference, Gallagher Estate, Midrand, 27 June 2007, in *New Agenda: South African Journal of Social and Economic Policy*, Issue 27.

NEDLAC (2003). Growth and Development Summit Agreement, June 2003.

Roberts, Simon (2009). 'Considerations for growth', August 2009.

Slovo, Joe (1976). 'South Africa – no middle road', in Basil Davidson, Joe Slovo & Anthony Wilkinson, 1976, *Southern Africa: the new politics of revolution*. Harmondsworth: Penguin Books.

Chapter 10
Competing Centres of Power

What is power like in an advanced capitalist country – for example, the United Kingdom? I identify four centres of power: the capitalist class and its power; the state system (because there is a public service and the security service); Cabinet and Parliament; and then the governing party. Each of those categories has power. The question is, how is power used? In whose interests, and with what consequences?

Let me start with the capitalist class. If we take the UK as an example, firstly the capitalist class in the UK controls and owns the means of production. In *The Communist Manifesto*, Marx and Engels said that the executive of the modern state is but a committee for managing the common affairs of the whole bourgeoisie. For decades afterwards, communists and progressives believed, above all, that the state in advanced capitalism was a coercive instrument of the ruling class. The argument was that because there was a bourgeoisie, with the capitalist class owning and controlling the means of production, this gave them an enormously powerful base in the system, which enabled them to use the state for its interest. I give the example of Margaret Thatcher, who used the police to smash the National Union of Mineworkers (NUM) during the 1984–85 coal miners' strike. Thereafter the union movement in Britain was much weaker. This is a very good example of how the capitalist class will use the state as a coercive means of production.

In his book *The State in Capitalist Society*, the British Marxist academic Ralph Miliband has made a very strong case that the capitalist class does not govern. The suggestion was that powerful capitalists could pick up the phone and say to the prime minister, 'do this and that', and he would do it. There was a simplistic view that the capitalist class was actually governing through the state. Miliband argues, and very persuasively, that the capitalist class does not govern. It uses the state, but it doesn't govern.

So, what does it do? Miliband says that the capitalist class doesn't need to govern because it has massive power outside the state. When Jackson Mthembu issued a document on the debate about the proposed press tribunal, he said that the ownership and control of the media reflect the racialist, class and gender character of our system. He suggested that the press supports the interest of the bourgeoisie of the capitalist class. In other words, the capitalist class doesn't need to govern because it has a massive preponderance outside the state.

What is that influence? It is an ideological influence, it is a lobby influence, and it operates through religious institutions, which are influenced by the capitalist class, as well as through the universities, intellectuals, the press and the education system. For instance, in the UK the education system tends to articulate the position that capitalism is a good system. The monarchy in England is certainly a pillar of capitalist society. Even among the religious institutions there is a respect – you go to church and you talk about God and Queen. The argument is that the capitalist class has so much influence outside the state that they don't need to govern directly. They govern indirectly through the ideological hegemony they establish outside the state – through the economy and through this indirect influence and all these different institutions. You've got all sorts of institutions – the professions, the Bar, the lawyers' councils, engineering councils, and so on – all of which support and uphold capitalism. The capitalist class is quite content, and they do not need to sit in Downing Street. According to Miliband, that power, outside the state, is decisive.

Then he talks about the state system as a whole, which includes the public service and the security service. Certainly in the UK you will not get a public servant, or certainly a senior one, criticising capitalism. He or she would be fired. So no one in the army or the police or the security services or senior levels of public service will criticise capitalism. Why should the capitalists go into the public service? They don't need to. The system supports capitalism.

As I've indicated before, the public service – especially the security services – maintains social order. The miners' strike is not the only example; there have been many cases where trade unions, NGOs, anti-war movements, peaceniks etc. go and demonstrate in the streets and the police maintain order in the interests of the existing system, which of course is a capitalist system. Furthermore, the public service articulates social democracy as an ideology. If you go to a public service school or a police college, what they are taught is that you maintain social order – law and order. At one time I did some teaching of the British police and I can tell you this: the job of the police, the army, the public service and all the state institutions is to maintain law and order and respect for the law.

But even as the state and its institutions support capitalism, it also has a certain relative autonomy. You'll find that in the UK and in many other countries, the public service begins to develop a human face and they begin to improve the health services, education system and certain social conditions. It has therefore a relative autonomy. It can act with a certain amount of independent discretion within the overall framework of a capitalist society. So the public service is free to institute various reforms that give the state a human face – showing that it loves people, is good to the people and is doing all kinds of welfare things. That's the UK system.

The Cabinet and Parliament exercise policy, take many decisions and legislate. On the whole in the UK, the legislation and the policies that come out of Cabinet and Parliament support capitalism. There is no party in the British Parliament that is against capitalism. The Labour Party and the Liberal Democrats are fully behind capitalism. In the UK and in Europe generally and in the United States, the Cabinet, the executive, the Parliament, the Congress, all support capitalism. There's no need for the capitalist class to be in Parliament because they are able to handle the system through indirect links.

When it comes to the governing party, Ralph Miliband argues that Parliament and the political party system have diminished in importance. He says the political parties play only a subordinate role in the whole system of power. According to Miliband, that is the situation in the advanced capitalist countries.

Turning to South Africa, what are the parallels and what are the differences? Firstly, in South Africa, what does the capitalist do? I think we all know that the capitalist class does not govern directly in South Africa. Secondly, they own and control the means of production. Thirdly, they use the state and they influence the state. In South Africa, they use BEE as a kind of camouflage mechanism. That's what they do, but they do not exercise decisive power.

There is an anxiety in the ANC that the press and various other channels – including our universities and in some cases the school system and the religious institutions – press the ideas of the capitalist class. If we look at public debate in South Africa, you can see the ideas of capitalist ideology even in the articulation of some Cabinet documents. Within the movement, the press and many other institutions, capitalist influences are quite strong; therefore, as in the UK and the US, the capitalist class exercises influence outside the state system in a big way. I'm not sure whether those influences are decisive or not. I think we always talk about a balance of forces, including a balance of ideological forces. There's a battle going on in South Africa, and I would argue this battle is much more severe than in the UK, where there is broad national agreement that capitalism is a good system. In South Africa we don't have that broad national agreement.

In my view, the capitalist class does not govern in South Africa. It owns and controls the means of production, just as in the UK. It influences and uses the state, but I would say that the capitalist class does not have decisive power in South Africa. Of course, I argue that they use all sorts of mechanisms to push the ideology of capitalism.

Now, what about the state in South Africa? What are the differences between us and the UK? This state maintains the existing system. If the ANC decides to change the social order one day, then the public service has to defend the new social order. Under Stalin, the Soviet regime maintained the existing order. In China, the public service, the army and the police maintain the existing order. In the US, the state maintains the existing order. In South Africa, the state also tries to articulate the idea of national unity, the rainbow nation; our President and our leaders are always talking about the need for national unity. Even here, the state has relative autonomy. Our state system can do certain things without asking permission from the capitalist class. Here in Parliament we pass laws, which are sometimes against the interests of the capitalist class. So we have relative autonomy as the state. We're able to introduce reforms of all kinds.

There are quite a number of parallels between our system and the advanced capitalist system, but I think there are also differences. What is the role of Cabinet and Parliament in South Africa? Firstly, our Cabinet makes policy. Secondly, the Cabinet and Parliament take decisions, but we do not support the inherited system. In the UK, the Cabinet and Parliament are designed to maintain the inherited system – the House of Lords, the structures of the civil service, the whole feudal atmosphere in which the inherited system of Britain's democracy is maintained. Here in South Africa the language is different. We attack apartheid all the time.

In South Africa we talk about a mixed economy, which is why some of us take exception to people saying that our economy is essentially capitalist. We are in favour of state-owned enterprises and cooperatives. There is a push within the ANC towards a mixed economy, which is not fundamentally perpetuating capitalism as a system.

According to Miliband, the governing party plays a smaller role in the totality of power. The Alliance – the ANC, COSATU and SACP – has a much different field to it in relation to power. There is a struggle for power by the Alliance, which we don't find in advanced capitalism. The Conservative Party in the UK is not essentially geared to a change of the system; they want to perpetuate the system. The Democratic Party and the Republican Party in the US similarly defend the existing system.

In South Africa the ANC is the ruling party – note the distinction between ruling party and a governing party. The ANC has a tradition of struggle. Crude as it is, that's the position. Also, as the ruling party in advanced capitalism, on the whole the ANC, COSATU and the SACP have ideological power, which is not to sustain capitalism. Thabo Mbeki, in a speech some years ago, said that the ANC is not a socialist party. I think this is understood, but we're also not a capitalist party. The social democratic parties in Europe and North America are overtly capitalist parties. Nobody can assert that the ANC is a capitalist party. It is a broad church with an as-yet-unformed ideology. You can read Strategy and Tactics a hundred times and you cannot, in a simple formula, say that the ANC has a certain ideological position. Unlike the Conservative Party in the UK, and even the Labour Party, the ruling party in South Africa has a base in the working class. It's true at the moment. It looks a bit shaky, but essentially the ruling party in South Africa has historically deep roots in the working class.

Finally, unlike bourgeois parties in Europe and North America, this ruling party constantly talks about having deep roots in the masses. The ANC is a mass-based party. We can't say the same about capitalist parties in Europe. I think there is a fundamental difference between the way a bourgeois or parliamentary party in Europe or in the US views itself and its role and how we see the ANC. I believe that there are many similarities between the capitalist state and the capitalist system of power, but there are also differences.

To sum up very quickly, in advanced capitalism you have a strong capitalist class which does not govern. It doesn't need to govern because the people who are doing the governing are governing in their interests – in the interests of capitalism or monopoly capitalism. The press, churches, schools, universities and public service in some way maintain social order and the existing system of capitalism.

In South Africa the capitalist class also does not govern, and I would argue that it has less power here than the same class in the UK. The capitalist class in South Africa also uses outside forces, but I believe that that power is not decisive. The key word is 'decisive'. Similarly, the public service in South Africa supports the existing system, but it does so in a reformist manner. We are working in an incremental system where there are reforms, and the public service introduces those reforms, albeit with different degrees of enthusiasm. The Cabinet and Parliament in South Africa are really quite different from their counterparts in the UK or the United States. Our Cabinet opposes the inherited system and the naked power of capitalism. It tries to control and regulate it, with a limited degree of success. The character of the state in South Africa is different to some degree to that in advanced capitalism. The biggest difference is the nature of the governing party in advanced capitalism and the ruling party in South Africa. Here, the ruling party has a far different feel, vision, agenda and ideological approach. It also has far stronger links with the working class and the masses.

So, it cannot be said that the ruling party in South Africa is weak or indecisive. On the contrary, our ruling party could, if it decides to do so, become decisive. We've not yet decided to be decisive, whereas in Britain and in the US political parties are not decisive and are unlikely to become so. That is one of the key differences between the two systems.

Chapter 11
Political Economy

The focus of this chapter will be political economy. My intention is to broaden the discussion undertaken in Chapter 9 on the politics of economics. Why political economy? Karl Marx was a political economist, and *Das Kapital*, his major work, was called the theory of political economy. Before Marx, there was Adam Smith and David Ricardo – classical economists who understood the link between politics and economics. Unfortunately today bourgeois economists don't like that link, and universities teach either politics or economics, not political economy.

First, there are four terms that must be defined; these are social formation, mode of production, forces of production and relations of production. Marx's whole theory was based on those four terms. Basically, what they said was that in any social formation (a system of society), there are different modes of production. For instance, in South Africa, we have the capitalist mode of production, but in the rural areas there is also a survivalist economy, which is not capitalism as such. Capitalism has penetrated the rural areas, but it really developed in Johannesburg with the rise of the mining industry. In the rural areas, there was an almost tribal society, which was not capitalist, and the two modes of production lived together in one social formation for a while until the migrant labour system destroyed that.

What is a social formation? A social formation is another word for society.

What is a mode of production? It's the way that an economy is organised.

What are the forces of production? The forces of production include the finance in an economy, as well as the technology, the skills, labour and markets. In capitalism the forces of production include finance, high technology, skilled labour, engineers, designers and technologists.

According to Marx, the relations of production refer primarily to class relations: the capitalist class, the working class and the middle strata. The relations of production are the relations between the owners of the means of production and the controllers of the means of production and those who work in the system.

The theory of Marxism was set out very clearly in *The Communist Manifesto*, which Marx co-wrote with Friedrich Engels. The pamphlet was two things. Firstly, it was a political programme. Marx wanted to start a communist movement. He failed, because it took many years before the first communist party was formed. *The Communist Manifesto* is on the one hand a political programme; on the other hand it is a theory of capitalism.

Before Marx, philosophers in Europe believed that there was a thought system called dialectic, where you have the thesis, the antithesis and the synthesis. For instance, if someone says we must nationalise the mines, that's a thesis. Another person says the market is much better. That's an antithesis: there's a conflict between those two ideas. Then you consider whether it is possible to nationalise the mines within capitalism or a mixed economy, and you develop a new idea of how you can combine two ideas, which at first seemed to be in conflict. That idea is the synthesis.

I think that's what's happening at the moment. I was recently at a meeting in Gauteng: on the panel was Floyd Shivambu and Zwelinzima Vavi, and there was immediate conflict between them on the question of nationalisation. But after discussion, something began to emerge on how we can tackle this issue in a positive way. So the idea is that a *thesis*, which is a proposition, and an *antithesis*, which is the opposite, can become something new in a *synthesis*. Marxism was rooted in a philosophical idea that you can combine two opposites into something new. Mao Tse-tung spoke about antagonistic and non-antagonistic contradictions. Marx said that in society classes are antagonistic, and it is very difficult to live with the two together in a non-antagonistic way. He said that class struggle is the motive force of change.

Marx said that classes have existed since the earliest times, even in tribal society. However, it was with slavery that class antagonisms really developed. There is a very severely antagonistic, hostile class contradiction between slaveowners and slaves. Feudalism, the system under which lords owned vast amounts of land while serfs worked their lands, represented another example of class contradiction.

Marx argued that the antagonism between the capitalist and the workers would intensify. He predicted that the capitalist class would get smaller and more powerful and that the working class would get bigger and bigger and that the middle strata would fall down into the working class and create the foundations for a proletarian revolution. In *The Communist Manifesto*, Marx expected that the working class would soon rise and overthrow capitalism. However, it didn't happen. There was a wave of revolutionary uprisings across Europe in 1848, and a very big struggle of workers in France in the 1870s. It was only in 1917 in Russia that the proletarian revolution succeeded. Marx was wrong, and he was wrong on quite a few things.

One of the things we must note is that Marx and Lenin said that the proletarian revolution must first be a democratic revolution. Those of you who know your history will know that Russia underwent a democratic revolution in February

1917, not a socialist revolution. The socialist revolution came in October, and there were two, not one. In February 1917, an alliance of class forces established democracy and a Parliament, but things didn't work. In October came the uprising led by the Bolsheviks (a communist party), which created the socialist revolution.

Marx said that 'the communists do not form a separate party opposed to other working class parties. They do not set up any sectarian principles of their own. They bring to the front the common interest of the entire proletariat, independent of nationality; always and everywhere the communists represent the interest of the movement as a whole.' That was enormous foresight. What he was trying to say was that the communists should not break away and become separatist; they should be part of a bigger movement representing the whole.

Marx's original idea was that capitalism would break up and the rich would get richer and smaller in number, but the mass of the proletariat would get bigger and bigger and there would be no middle section. He was wrong about that, especially with the advent of imperialism in Latin America, Africa and elsewhere. I think many Marxists, in the later period, would say that capitalism was saved by colonial exploitation. Lenin wrote about this. For instance, what capitalists did in Britain was to use the exploitation of the colonies, the wealth of the colonies, to pay off British workers. Essentially, British capitalism survived on the basis of wealth extracted from overseas colonies, particularly from India and Africa.

The same thing happened in South Africa. When the mines were first developed, white workers were also paid badly. Of course, migrant black workers were paid very badly. White workers organised unions and went on strike – for example, in 1922 – which prompted the ruling class to offer concessions. Even the Union government of 1910 gave massive concessions to white workers in order to keep them quiet. So the system of buying off the upper level of the working class to keep them happy flourished in South Africa.

So you've got the forces of production, like finance, skills, technology and so on in a capitalist country. As growth takes place, with it go the relations of production, the differences between capitalists and workers, as well as the tensions and the contradictions between those two. These contradictions should lead to proletarian revolution, according to Marx. That is how history works. That is the theory.

Responses to questions

Why did Marx and Lenin say that the democratic stage comes first? The main reason was that the social forces were not right at the time. For instance, in Europe there was no communist party in 1848 at the time of *The Communist Manifesto*. Marx said communism arose but there were no parties. There were social democratic movements and such things. In fact, the first parties to become communists were called social democrats. The literature of Lenin is full of social democracy. In 1903, the Social Democratic Party of Russia split into the Bolsheviks and Mensheviks – the majority and minority, respectively. For instance, the Communist Party of the Soviet Union (CPSU) had 'Bolshevik' in brackets after it to show that they were the majority. Both Marx and Lenin felt that although capitalism creates huge contradictions between the capitalist class and the working class or proletariat, that doesn't mean that the proletariat is ready to make the socialist revolution. Frankly, if you said to me that the majority of the proletariat in South Africa was ready for a socialist revolution in 1994, I don't think most of us would agree with you. That's why the ANC went into the settlement and established a democratic state. The first change must be a democratic change, in which you involve large masses of people who are not communists, who don't understand communism.

Contradiction in society

The reason that the October Revolution happened, the socialist revolution, which was led by the communist party and the Soviets, was because the country was in chaos. The February Revolution brought to power a mixture of democrats, social democrats, communists, workers and middle elements and that failed to produce anything. Don't forget it was during the First World War, with chaos, poverty and hunger everywhere, especially in the rural areas but also in the cities. The first revolution did not solve anything. So the communists said, this is chaotic, let's move in and take power and they were able to do it because of the chaos. You need chaos before you make revolution. This is the essence of Marxism. Marx, Lenin and Engels understood that you can't make revolution by excitement. There has to be a contradiction in society. The ANC must confront that. We call ourselves revolutionary, a disciplined force of the left, NDR, and so on, and you look around you and you say, where is this revolution? You must study the contradictions in a society before you get excited. Yes, you can talk theory, which is what I'm talking now, but the contradictions have not yet developed, and you can't make them develop by yourself. You can teach, you can argue, but you can't make contradictions. They come in the political economy of a society.

The bourgeois classes

As the two bourgeois classes, or the capitalist class, separate from the proletariat as the contradiction grows bigger, a small section of the ruling class cuts itself adrift and joins the revolutionary class. Even though there's the separation between the classes, a small section of the ruling class joins the revolutionary class. I come from the privileged white middle class; my father was a businessman, a manufacturer. When I was a student, I joined the movement. There were others like me, like Joe Slovo, Ruth First and Bram Fischer. We joined the movement even though we came from the bourgeois class. Marx said in 1848 that this is what's going to happen. Those of you who are 'Africanist' or 'blackist' or 'sectarian' and think that South Africa is only an African country are making a big mistake. If there are whites, coloureds and Indians who want to join the revolutionary movement, allow it; it's good because they bring something. If any of you are sectarian and think that all the bourgeois are forever uninformed, Marx said don't worry, some of them will break away, and often it's intellectuals who break away.

The role of the state

One of the things that Marx began to study was the role of the state. Marx said 'the executive of the modern state is but a committee for managing the common affairs of the whole bourgeoisie'. In the modern state, the executive is the government, particularly the Cabinet. The Cabinet is the committee that manages the whole country. The common affairs are the problem of all, of the whole bourgeoisie, not only the owners of the means of production. The important word here is 'common', and I'll tell you why. After Marx, communists and theoreticians in Europe began to say that the capitalists control the state. Some of you may remember there were comrades in the movement who said that Oppenheimer controls what the National Party does, and that Oppenheimer is the real power in South Africa. There were comrades in the movement who were saying don't worry about the National Party, Oppenheimer is the real enemy. Even in the days of Marx, that was a mistake, because the state does not manage the affairs of the top capitalists. They manage the common affairs of the whole bourgeoisie. Why did Marx say that? In later years, Marxist political theorists began to analyse how the state works and how business works, and the links between them. What these theorists discovered, by analysing capitalism in Britain and in the advanced countries, is that the capitalist class does not govern. Marx understood that. The modern state isn't actually sitting in the Cabinet. What the capitalists do is establish a complex system in which they don't need to make that phone call. Yes, they network, they do create linkages, but the state has what is called relative autonomy. What is the link between the state, business and capitalist class? It's an indirect relationship. That's what Marx was saying.

Did Marx believe that at some stage there would be a classless society in which there would be no class contradictions?
Absolutely. In *The Communist Manifesto*, Marx and Engels end off by saying that the proletarian revolution would fight not for its own interests alone, but for the interests of the whole of society. The key is the means of production. Under capitalism, feudalism and slavery, you've got the contradiction of class between the owners of the means of production and the workers. Marx argued that the proletariat does not own the means of production, and that when the proletariat takes power it would ensure that there would no longer be a conflict between the ownership of the means of production and society. Therefore, in time you would move towards a classless society. He was wrong, because what happened in the Soviet Union – and maybe we're beginning to see it in South Africa – is that despite the revolution, a new class comes into being which usurps state power. In the Soviet Union the bureaucracy became a new class; they did not own the means of production directly, so they were not capitalists, but they made sure that the system favoured them and not the masses.

Chapter 12

BEE Transactions and
Their Unintended Consequences

The empowerment transactions of Black Economic Empowerment (BEE) have taken centre stage in the debate about South Africa's future. There are accusations of cronyism, enrichment, parasitism and other pejorative labels. These transactions need to be analysed objectively to assess what is really going on, and they have to be seen in the broader trajectory of government objectives.

The ANC has been pursuing a 'democratic revolution' for fifty years. The main content of this has been the removal of white minority domination and the promotion of the liberation of black people, especially the black African majority. For much of this time, the expectation was that the democratic revolution would open the road to some form of socialism. But the world has changed, and the system of capitalism has acquired immense resilience throughout the world. Hence the ANC and the government are seeking other means to empower the black African majority in the economy.

Even a cursory examination of the various BEE Charters and Codes reveals a profound determination to deracialise the economy and ensure that black Africans in particular have a powerful presence throughout the economy, including its largest corporations. This amounts to a social revolution by administrative means. The immediate prospects are that it will succeed. However, there are unintended consequences in that the values of capitalism are now hegemonic throughout the society, and a new black business class is in formation. Although most of these individuals have political credentials, they are now focused on personal wealth through equity ownership accumulation and capital growth in private companies, leaving the redress of social issues to the state.

At the heart of the BEE process is a frantic deal-making process, whereby black businesspeople seek to enter the previously exclusive terrain of white capital. This chapter attempts to examine these 'empowerment transactions' and their unintended consequences for the political economy of South Africa. Whether the government will be able to sustain its commitment to the goals of a shared economy and society in the light of these developments is the subject of another debate.

Recent reports show that the unfolding of the BEE process is causing some concern. There seems to be a great deal of turbulence in the business world as black partners acquire shares in various companies while others move into short-term business opportunities. Since the country is committed to BEE and a great deal of effort is going into creating Charters and Codes, it is in the public interest that we develop a better understanding of what is going on in these empowerment transactions.

The deracialisation of top positions in large companies is a widely accepted goal. But is this mere tokenism, or is real power and influence actually acquired by black partners? Is black influence being acquired, and at what price? We also need to understand whether middle-level black professionals are also given opportunities for advancement and exposure under the black empowerment process.

Do the black partners acquire net assets (equity) in the process, and is this immediate or is there a delay of many years? Is it the case that only a handful have actually been enriched while the rest have acquired only massive debts in the hope of rich pickings in the future? What are the actual material benefits for those who become directors of large companies?

We need to know what commitments follow from their roles as BEE partners. Assuming that the companies concerned are not acting out of charity, what benefits do these companies expect out of their divestment of shares to BEE partners? Is it political influence? Access to government departments? It is the lack of clarity about these matters that prompted *Time* magazine to put Cyril Ramaphosa on its cover (6 June 2006) with the caption 'The New Rand Lords: Capitalists or Cronies?'

Many of these individuals are highly talented, with a long record of public service, first in the liberation struggle, then in various roles in the public domain. Yet they appear to be wholly engrossed in deal-making to boost their personal business affairs and have given up any public role. Most no longer contribute to providing direction to the country as a whole, and this is a great loss. But for those who would choose to remain active in the political life of the country, what degree of political freedom do they retain, as BEE partners, to keep their struggle values?

It may be that the whole exercise needs review so that the country loses fewer of its most distinguished black personalities to the pursuit of perhaps illusory enrichment. Of course, it can be argued that we need black businesspeople in the top echelons of business to deracialise it and influence its direction, but experience thus far gives little support to the idea that the present method is effective.

The background

Black economic empowerment (BEE) was designed as a mechanism for the deracialisation of wealth and economic power in South Africa. This was in line with the Freedom Charter's objective that 'the people shall share in the country's wealth.' But the means of doing so were always unclear, perhaps leaning towards the model of the social democratic countries of Europe, which used some public ownership, some semi-autonomous parastatals, a welfare state, heavy taxation of the rich, scope for strong unionism to raise workers wages, cooperatives, etc.

The government realised that these aspirations were unlikely to be achieved without state intervention. However, rigorous measures such as nationalisation were thought to be unrealistic. Instead, a process of drawing up BEE Empowerment Charters was begun by former deputy president Phumzile Mlambo-Ngcuka when she was the Minister for Minerals and Energy. Several other sectors have now followed suit, although each industry has followed a different path.

The Mining Charter seeks to give 'real benefits to all' and to realise 'the promise of a non-racial South Africa'. It seeks to encourage black economic empowerment, transformation at the tiers of ownership, management, skills development, employment equity, procurement and rural development: 'The transfer of ownership must take place in a transparent manner and for fair market value.' It proposes that ownership of a business can come through a majority shareholding, joint venture or partnerships, or broad-based ownership. The ultimate ten-year objective is to achieve a 26 per cent share of ownership by historically disadvantaged persons. The government is to play an important role in overseeing and facilitating the process and there are many reporting requirements.

The Financial Sector Charter follows a similar route, but stresses that participation is voluntary. There are many detailed clauses, including a targeted procurement strategy to enhance BEE by procuring from black companies. There is also a commitment to joint ventures, debt financing and equity investment in BEE companies. Another requirement is for 'appropriate risk-mitigating measures and risk-sharing arrangements between government and its Development Finance Institutions and the private sector'. There are many targets and reporting systems. These include a target of 33 per cent black people on the boards of directors by 2008 and a minimum of 25 per cent black people at executive level by 2008. These measures alone will bring a social revolution in business in this country.

The Tourism Charter is even more detailed, with complex scorecards. The Petroleum and Liquid Fuels Industry Charter deals with procurement issues as well as state tender matters. The Maritime Transport and Services BEE Strategy raises more long-term issues about the performance of the economy, including creating a larger market, legislative and fiscal restrictions, commitment by parastatals and public-sector organisations, with much emphasis on 'accelerating procurement from black-owned and empowered enterprises'.

In short, in each of these Charters the concessions to enable BEE are combined with some hard-nosed negotiations for concessions from government for the private sector. The targets are very ambitious, and may well run up against limitations on human capacity. They can only be achieved if there is a huge change of attitude in business to the role of black people in general.

The Codes of Good Practice issued by the Department of Trade and Industry (DTI) are even more ambitious and extremely complex. It will take a small army of lawyers and accountants to interpret them for business and the general public. How Parliament is to exercise oversight remains to be seen.

Deracialising the economic heights

The *Sunday Times* survey of wealth and corporate ownership (21 December 2005) showed that there had been little transfer of wealth to black individuals and companies despite BEE and the Charters. Of the top earners, only the names of Jacob Modise (Johnnic Holdings), Phuthuma Nheko (CEO, MTN), Sizwe Nxasana (CEO, Telkom) and Irene Charnley (MTN) can be identified as previously disadvantaged people. That is 4 out of 70. Of the wealthiest, we find Patrice Motsepe, Desmond Lockey, Tokyo Sexwale, Reuel Khoza, Marcel Golding, Anant Singh, Jens Montanana, Saki Macozoma and Mikki Xayiya as obviously previously disadvantaged people. That is 9 out of 157 individuals.

Why is this so? What is really happening? Are we seeing any real deracialising of wealth and economic power? Or is it all smoke and mirrors? One investment analyst has suggested that 'everyone is now in the game', but that many corporates see BEE as an unpleasant and unnecessary tax-compliance cost. The same analyst says that black people without capital are hastily and rashly either fronting, borrowing from ruthless lenders or otherwise getting in way over their heads. The stock exchange will need to rise over 500 per cent for some of these aspirants to realise any return. So, while a few have made it and have net assets, much is a mirage. He also believes that the government is sitting back and allowing it to happen, and is not taking seriously enough the potential for massive failures if interest rates rise and debt cannot be paid off. Such concerns are sufficiently serious to be examined rigorously and objectively, without ideological overtones.

Deal-making

It is vital that we have a clear understanding of what is happening in our economy, who is benefiting, and whether there are any real prospects of transformation at the top of the pile. If we do not do so, some will make unsubstantiated accusations of elite self-serving practices, of rapid class polarisation, of the entrenching of a new capitalist class, and so on. Others will continue to bemoan the enrichment of the black elite. The true state of class behaviour will remain a mystery.

Some of the key questions that need answers are as follows:

- What is the extent of actual net wealth and assets held by the black business elite?
- What actual economic muscle do they have?
- To what extent has BEE empowered these people?

- What is their ideological orientation?
- What prospects are there that they will use their wealth/ power to transform the economy?
- To what extent has BEE opened the way for sharing/ redistribution of the country's wealth?
- What conflict of interests has this created, and at what cost?

In an article in *Business Day* (16 January 2006) Tim Cohen argues that 'the vast majority of shareholders in the original deal [for Johnnic Holdings] were left with nothing.' Yet Johnnic was a treasure trove of assets with a total market capitalisation of R8.5 billion in 1996. The purchase price was R50 per share, i.e. a 6 per cent discount. Cohen concludes that the price was on the high side, and that very few of the assets were under direct control of management. It was a 'classic apartheid-era mess'. He goes on to say that the lenders held all the aces since the deal was essentially debt-financed. It was 'theoretically value-creating'; using 'convertible cumulative redeemable preference shares, funders took none of the downside and gave very little of the upside. There was no upside anyway.' And so 'the saga produced little success, since companies are hard to run if their investors are hopelessly indebted to the banks.'

What is required is a thorough understanding of the mechanisms of share transfer to BEE beneficiaries, what the actual benefits amount to, and what are the consequent obligations on the potential beneficiary. To what extent are they obliged to use their former and ongoing connections in the ANC and government to win procurement orders, get contracts and influence government programmes? Is the National Treasury happy with this process, and does the Auditor General approve? Is there a conflict of interest for senior public servants and ministers due to the involvement of relatives?

On the other hand many of the key individuals involved in these deals are quite confident that they can make a difference.

In *Time* magazine, Saki Macozoma said: 'With five or six of us spread out through the economy, that can make a difference in a fundamental way' (*Time*, 6 June 2005).

Key questions

Why do companies do it? Not all the black partners have business experience. There is a view that there are considerable penalties, that 'most BEE transactions destroy shareholder value' (*Business Report*, 10 January 2006). Some argue that they find it essential to bring black faces to the top for image reasons.

According to *Time* (6 June 2005): 'As South Africa's biggest companies rushed to meet their BEE requirements, they often turned to the same small group of black capitalists, offering to sell or grant equity stakes at favourable terms, often financed by the companies themselves, in return for connections, expertise and links to the marketplace.'

Cyril Ramaphosa took a different line. He argued that 'black South Africans need to get their hands on capital or they won't be able to build anything – first you become a financial investor to accumulate capital ... then you acquire skills ... then you acquire control of companies and begin to be an operator, running a proper business' (*Time*, 6 June 2005).

In 2006, Mvela Resources, another major empowerment company, seemed to be reviewing its role. It now wished to control the assets it had invested in (*Business Report*, 10 January 2006). In another report (*Business Day*, 10 January 2006), Mvela appeared to contemplate selling its 15 per cent stake in Gold Fields, because it did not own a controlling stake. But then ownership would 'only vest in five years' time'. Mvela's investor relations manager stated that Mvela Resources would have about R2 billion in debt by 2009, 'which could be repaid by selling some Gold Fields shares'. An analyst said: 'Mvela Resources was not yet entitled to the shares and it would not be easy to enter into any arrangements to sell them at this stage.'

Some propositions

To guide our investigation we start with several propositions:

- BEE in the form of a transfer of shares is a mechanism for delayed transfer of wealth linked purely to expediential company performance and with no downside or cost to the company.
- Wealth transfer from historically white companies requires total loyalty and commitment from new black junior partners.
- This loyalty requires crony conduct with government.
- The ANC may be compromised by such conduct on the part of respected personalities.

Empowerment transactions

A typical case might be as follows. A large company decides that it is politically expedient to take on a black partner. It identifies a suitable person with a high public profile. It offers this person a stake in the company equity and requires a small payment. The individual has no funds, so takes a loan from a bank, which is secured by the shares. The actual transfer of the shares is made conditional on the performance of the company and the value of shares on the stock exchange. Also there is a time-frame of, say, five years before the actual transfer can take place. In the meanwhile, the individual may be offered a seat on the board, for which he will draw non-executive attendance fees and will benefit from dividends. In return for these immediate benefits, he has to assist with obtaining government tenders and generally improving the company's image as one committed to BEE. In other words, he is controlled by 'golden handcuffs'. The company remains in the control of the main shareholders, who dictate its overall economic policy. If for some reason the individual leaves, he will typically lose his investment stake and any upside that may already have built up – it is all or nothing.

There are many variations on this model, including ones where the beneficiary has to put up his personal assets, such as his house, as security. One important feature is that the beneficiary is given enough funds to acquire a lifestyle commensurate with his new status. This leads to the impression that a new black capitalist class has emerged. In fact there is a high degree of 'capture', which undermines the individual's capacity to play a significant role in the economic transformation of the country.

Our early enquiries indicated that there are at least three types of BEE candidates, each with a distinct role:

1. Entrepreneurial groups
   * Former politicians with a high public profile.
   * Others well connected with government.
   * Skilled professionals with expertise at running businesses and who are also deal-makers. They often put together finance and run companies where appropriate. Wheeler-dealers who operate opportunistically are also part of this category.
2. Trade union investment groups
3. Broad-based groups, e.g. NGOs, foundations, etc.

Of these, the entrepreneurial groups are thought to have led to a great deal of entrepreneurial activity, with some successes, while the broad-based structures are said to have created little value and may be ineffective. Johnnic was such a scheme, which embraced many diverse entities.

The essence of empowerment transactions is that a group or individual with little capital wishes to acquire a stake in some existing company. The usual route is as follows:

* set up a company (or a trust)
* establish a 'special purpose vehicle' (SPV)
* seek to acquire shares in an existing company, say 'XX'.

Let us assume that the price of one share is R18. Where does the funding come from, since the trust has little ready cash? We can assume that the trust has some personal savings and can pay R1 per share. The bulk of the remainder comes from a bank, insurance company or any funding institution that is willing to advance finance, and pays R12 per share (it is similar to a bank overdraft). The remaining R5 is contributed by company XX. This contribution may in the form of a discount, a loan or a guarantee to some other funder providing a loan.

The BEE trust is of course beholden to others in the deal, especially to the facilitating company (XX), without whose intervention there is no hope of a deal. So BEE deals depend on the willingness of company XX. Company XX and the SPV measure the degree of risk against the expectation of a financial return. If the risk is great, the cost of the funding is high, and vice versa. The key question is, 'what value is added by the empowerment deal?' Or, 'what can this group bring to the party?'

Company XX has to make a judgment on whether the deal is worthwhile and who can put it together. It may be a former politician. This is because there is government pressure for visible empowerment. But empowerment that is cosmetic can be costly, and the company needs to remain profitable.

In the early days of BEE, business was not under much pressure to make empowerment deals. If they wished to improve their image, they might give a black company a small discount for share purchases. In such cases it was the banks that advanced the money, thereby taking most of the risk, so they demanded high interest rates on the loans. In 1995 national bank rates were high, at 16 per cent, so the banks wanted 25 per cent interest on these loans to cover the risk. The borrower depended on dividends or share value appreciation to repay the loan. However, there was a stock market crash in 1998 and the market remained flat until 2003. There was no share appreciation and interest rate repayments were high. So, with a few exceptions, the whole BEE experiment collapsed.

Since 2003, interest rates have fallen and the banks are asking 17 per cent. Furthermore, the JSE has risen by some 200 per cent, and shares have appreciated substantially. This makes for a rosy scenario. It is cheaper for the facilitator XX to fund the deal, as the risk premium is only 3 per cent, and the share price must only rise by 7 per cent (previously it was 25 per cent). This helps economic growth, and therefore share values rise. There has thus been a huge increase in the number of companies acting as facilitators. However, should interest rates rise again, and if there is a fall on the stock market, BEE will stall. But there is a built-in safeguard for the BEE group in that the SPV loan is ring-fenced, which means that the bank or finance house will face the loss, not the BEE group, who paid only a small amount upfront (R1 per share in our example).

What's in it for the company?

Public attention has thus far been mainly on the beneficiaries. But what's in it for company XX? One would expect that while some businesses might wish to gain some social responsibility scores, it is profit that really counts. So what value does BEE compliance bring?

Since much effort has gone into creating Charters and Codes, there is more inducement now for compliance with BEE intentions. It is of course possible to do so in a tokenist way, but there is too much public interest for blatant violations of the process. Furthermore, there is enormous pressure from aspirant black candidates, which is building up social momentum. Business as a whole will have to give some ground. Good points can be scored there. BEE deals can bring new opportunities for established companies – for instance, in mining.

The kinds of BEE partners that are favoured are those with inside knowledge in government. These personalities also have easy access to ministers and top officials, with the golf circuit a favourite contact point. There is a great deal of socialising among top people in government and business, and informal talk may be a great asset. In the US it is called 'schmoozing', and it brings in a great deal of business. BEE partners are also much more adept at internal transformation to meet representivity criteria and to change the corporate culture of businesses. This is invaluable in the current climate. BEE partners are also able to bring new knowledge of the market culture, especially with respect to the new black middle strata. They bring new business insights, new kinds of experience and skills.

However, the actual value added to a company depends on the proper criteria being put in place initially and the correct choice of a partner. Many an initial high expectation has failed to deliver because the wrong partner was chosen, the terms laid down were bad and the relationship managed inappropriately. This is clearly a matter for expert management. What is clear is that it is completely inadequate to place an ineffectual BEE partner on the board of directors, for window-dressing purposes, when that person cannot fulfil the duties involved, or to offer that person share options that are unrealistic. Too many new supposed beneficiaries come into a deal for the fast buck and not for commitment to the success of the company.

International investors

There is considerable concern by international companies about BEE, for fear that they will have to surrender equity to local partners. However Code 100, Statement 103, deals with the 'recognition of ownership contributions made by multinational companies'. This Code makes provision for an 'equity equivalent' consisting of a public programme or scheme of government which allows a multinational company points under the Ownership Scorecard. Local multinational enterprises will have to show that they 'will suffer substantial commercial harm' if they implement BEE. Various other obligations may also be introduced.

For further enquiry

The issues that require detailed investigation are as follows:

- What is the package offered?
- What is the share incentivisation scheme?
- How is the scheme paid for?
- What are the terms of the scheme?
- How is it linked to the equity value of the company?
- What are the potential conflicts of interest?
- What is the effect on the national interest?
- What government contracts are affected?
- What legislation is affected?

Serious questions arise about how BEE impacts on the political system. On the assumption that the number of actual beneficiaries of BEE who hold senior positions in the ANC is very small, it may be assumed that their influence on the political direction of the movement is small. On the other hand, there is a new tendency for office bearers to become shareholders in various companies under BEE schemes, and this could create dual loyalties towards the ANC and the companies. It may also have an impact on the ideological outlook of the individuals concerned.

Sources

'The Auditor-General's good governance: independence, transparency and accountability'. Interview with Shauket Fakie, in *New Agenda: South African Journal of Social and Economic Policy* No. 21, March 2006.

'Ready To Spend'. Interview with Lesetja Kganyago, Director General, National Treasury, in *New Agenda: South African Journal of Social and Economic Policy* No 21, March 2006.

Balshaw, Tony & Jonathan Goldberg (2005). *Cracking broad-based black economic empowerment.* Cape Town: Human & Rousseau.

Convention on Combating Bribery of Foreign Public Officials in International Business Transaction. Organisation for Economic Cooperation and Development. Daffe/IME/BR (97) 20.

Department of Trade and Industry (DTI) (2006). Charters for the following sectors: Mining, Financial Sector, Tourism, Petroleum and Liquid Fuels, Maritime Transport and Services.

Department of Trade and Industry (DTI) (2005). Codes of Good Practice on Black Economic Empowerment, Phase One and Phase Two, November 2005.

Lewis, Hendrik Archie (2004). An assessment of financial and supply chain management outcomes in Western Cape public hospitals. Unpublished MA thesis, University of Stellenbosch.

Prevention Procurement Regulations (2001). Preferential Procurement Policy Framework Act, No 5 of 2000.

Republic of South Africa (1992). Corruption Act 94 of 1992. Pretoria: Government Printer.

Republic of South Africa (2004). Prevention and Combating of Corrupt Activities Act 12 of 2004. Available from http://www.info.gov.za/acts/2004/a12-04/index.html; accessed 22 December 2010.

Treasury Regulations, 21249, 31 May 2000, Public Finance Management Act, 1999.

Western Cape Provincial Government (undated). Preferential Procurement Policy for the Western Cape.

Chapter 13
Black Business: The Challenge of Managing Capitalism

President Mbeki has made many speeches since he took over the leadership of South Africa. Three stand out as landmarks: 'I am an African', 'two nations' and the recent Nelson Mandela Memorial Lecture, on 'getting rich'.

This recent speech is being discussed from three perspectives: as part of a manoeuvre around the succession debate, as an exercise in political ethics and as contribution to an analysis of capitalism.

It is understandable that in the present climate of speculation around the future presidency – first of the ANC and then of the country – that almost every action by a political leader is ascribed to some positioning or other of various potential candidates for either position. The problem is that all this speculation remains just that. Was the President making a negative point about the newly rich to exclude them from the race? There are no real facts to go on, and we are often left with just gossip and hot air. We need to be patient and allow the process to work itself out.

We are on firmer ground with respect to ethics. This was a powerful speech made in the presence of some of the black aspirant millionaires who have joined in the race for getting rich with enthusiasm and total commitment. Mbeki condemned the values of designer clothing, conspicuous consumption and copycat behaviour of the rich and powerful. It was not only moralising, however, for he attacked the foundation of this behaviour in market fundamentalism, with its philosophy of success through capitalist acquisitiveness and indifference to the rest. Coming from an intellectual in office, who has repeatedly conceded that South Africa remains a capitalist country, this was a statement of the highest significance.

What is more, although he laid out the specific background of the ANC coming to power in the context of a capitalist system of oppression and exploitation, he criticised the fact the 'individual acquisition of wealth' has become the 'very centre of the value system of our society as a whole'. This has displaced 'the values of human solidarity' which infused the oppressed people over the previous decades, if not centuries. He used some very emotive phrases to condemn this displacement of values, such as the destruction of 'kinship, neighbourhood, profession and creed', people who become 'atomistic and individualistic', 'Get rich! Get rich! Get rich!', 'designer labels', 'the value system of the capitalist market' and 'the most theatrical and striking public display of wealth'.

He argued that 'we must never allow that the market should be the principal determinant of the nature of our society. We should firmly oppose market fundamentalism.' He went on to ask 'whether we are not ineluctably progressing towards the situation when the centre cannot hold', 'where things fall apart', and we face 'the phenomenon of social conflict'.

Having experienced this bombshell of denunciation of capitalism, the movement has to pick itself up and say, 'What now?' We have inherited a highly distorted form of capitalism, with its legacy of racial inequality and concentrated economic power in white hands, and we claim to be a 'liberation movement of the exploited and oppressed', indeed 'a disciplined force of the Left', engaged in a 'revolutionary project'.

Yet, after twelve years in power, we remain one of the most divided countries in the world, with perhaps one of the highest proportions of unemployment, poverty and inequality, which seem to persist despite major efforts of government to provide relief to the underprivileged in the form of welfare grants, the social wage or direct interventions.

A great deal of effort is being put into black economic empowerment (BEE) and affirmative action, which are designed to deracialise the economy, especially the commanding heights, but all this is occurring within the framework of the market economy, which means the effective exclusion of the majority of the historically exploited and oppressed.

Even these measures seem to be mere palliatives, since of the 70 top earners only 4 are black, and of the 157 wealthiest only 9 are black. No doubt this is changing quite rapidly, but there is a long way to go. In any case, this process is producing exactly the kind of values President Mbeki was condemning. And, just as importantly, there are few indications that the beneficiaries of this process of enrichment, and possibly some empowerment, are willing to support an attack on capitalist fundamentalism, let alone on capitalism as a system.

Instead, we find a great deal of manipulation of the relationship between state and capital in order to extract as much benefit from the huge pile of state resources through the complex systems of tendering and procurement. The nasty head of crony capitalism is becoming ever more deeply entrenched, as the exposures of the Auditor General and the Public Service Commission reveal (*New Agenda*, Issue 21, 2006).

It would seem that the movement must now call upon the new middle strata to stand up and support the President in his urgent call for better values in the world of business and integrity in the public sector. There is something called 'the public good', which needs constant reinforcement if it is to become the dominant value in our society.

But enough about ethics. What are the implications of the speech for the fundamental structure of our society?

Apartheid was a system of internal colonialism, characterised by the domination and exploitation of black people by white capital and the state, and serving the interests of white capital and whites generally. The allegiance of the white working class was obtained by means of special privileges of income and status. This means that an analysis of the role of the ANC must be based on a political economy approach, which embraces race and class concepts, and not simply on the system of race discrimination and oppression. One very important dimension is that the negotiated settlement in CODESA left the economy in the control of the white minority.

Nevertheless the establishment of the democratic state, in which the ANC became the ruling party, led to a total restructuring of political structures, including the steady increase of the presence and power of progressive forces in the diverse institutions of the state, as well as substantial shifts within the social order. Due to the opening of economic space, many blacks swelled the ranks of the middle strata and some rose into the ranks of the bourgeoisie and capitalist class.

A prospect has emerged of some unity in action of black and white workers on class issues, as in the miners' strike in August 2005, where black and white unions struck jointly against the combined power of the gold mines. But the ANC has always had its base in the African working class and the poor masses, and they remain the major component of the motive forces for change. The black middle strata also continue to be an important component of the national movement, as well as some elements of black business although they are not equally articulate on the class interests of the poor.

The small number of blacks who have managed to enter the ranks of the bourgeoisie proper can be divided into businesspeople, top corporate managers and public sector corporate managers. Their ascent has the effect of beginning to deracialise the exercise of economic power. But independent black capitalists are still relatively few.

There is clearly an effort by white capital to provide some

space for black capital, a process which is encouraged by the policy of affirmative action and BEE, whereby the state provides substantial support to black business through tenders and procurement as well as the allocation of share capital in state-owned enterprises (*New Agenda*, Issue 22, 2006).

A major question arises as to whether this new black bourgeoisie, and in particular its business components, will advance the interests of the masses, or whether some components will become junior partners of white capital, which has become increasingly integrated into global capital. Alternatively, as it gains in strength, will black business develop its own identity as the core of a national bourgeoisie promoting progressive policies domestically and internationally?

The experience of decolonisation in most post-independence African countries is that colonial capital and the colonial state managed to create a comprador neocolonial class, which abandoned the social and economic objectives of the national liberation movement. Will the same happen in South Africa? Or will the power of the ANC as a national movement continue to embrace all, or most, black people, irrespective of class location, in the cause of overcoming white domination and establishing a non-racial democratic order which reduces the inherited inequalities and provides a decent life for all? That was at the heart of President Mbeki's speech.

In other words, will the ANC be able to sustain its character as a 'disciplined force of the Left' with the primary motive force 'the working class and the poor generally'? (Resolution of the ANC National General Council, 30 June 2005) Can this position be sustained within a capitalist economy? Especially one that is integrated into the world capitalist economy and subject to the same polarisation effects?

Much depends on the conduct of the ANC itself. President Mbeki made an unusually strong critical statement on this subject at the National General Council on 3 July 2005:

Our historic victory has put our movement into a position of political power. Since 1994, the 82nd year of the existence of our movement, our people have mandated us to assume the position of a ruling party. To be a ruling party means that we have access to state resources. It means that those who want to do business with the state have to interact with those who control state power, the members of our movement who serve in government.

It means that those of us who serve in the organs of state have the possibility to dispense patronage. It therefore means that we have the possibility to purchase adherents, with no regard to the principles that are fundamental to the very nature of the African National Congress. All this makes control of state power a valuable asset. It makes membership of the ANC an easy route of access to state power. It makes membership of the ANC an attractive commercial proposition. It makes financial support for the ANC an investment for some of those who want to generate profits for themselves by doing business with government. (ANC National General Council, Pretoria, 3 July 2005)

But whatever the prospects of potential distortion within the state system, there are other important dynamics in the socio-economic system as a whole. The disturbing feature of the present scenario is that with a Gini coefficient at 0.70, income inequalities remain the same as, or even higher than, under apartheid when the Gini coefficient was 0.6 (1993). This means that the same degree of surplus extraction or economic exploitation of the masses remains in place (Turok, 2005a).

Over the past ten years, directors' fees have increased at an average rate of 29 per cent, non-executive directors (where many blacks are now appointed) by 49 per cent, while workers increased their incomes by 6.5 per cent (Labour Research Service annual report, 2004). Also, the conspicuous consumption on the part of the black bourgeoisie indicates a strong propensity to enjoy the same fruits as their white counterparts. There has been an 'increase in black affluence – 41 per cent of the affluent are now Africans' (Burger, 2004), while 60 per cent of the middle class is now black (Hirsch, 2004). (Rigorous data is not available.)

Blacks are clearly joining the white elite, which is one of the wealthiest in the world. South Africa had 690 'ultra-high-gross-worth individuals in 2002 with assets totalling $30 million each. There are 25 000 dollar millionaires living in South Africa with $300 billion in private wealth. Interestingly, the super-rich, people worth more than R200 million, have grown fourfold since 1994 (World Wealth Report, 2003, and VIP Forum, quoted in the *Sunday Times*, 9 May 2004).

A progressive black business class?

The case for encouraging the emergence of a black business class is compelling. Under apartheid, blacks were denied any scope for capital accumulation by a maze of restrictive legislation, a lack of skills and education, no access to loans and job reservation for skilled whites. It is therefore logical that a national liberation movement should insist that space be created for black capitalists in the interests of deracialising the economy. Also, many of the leading personalities in black business were leading figures in the ANC, and retain those links. The problem is that they come empty-handed onto the field; they are 'capitalists without capital'. After eight years of effort, black business had only captured between 1 and 4 per cent of the shares on the Johannesburg Stock Exchange (Southall, 2005:461).

Nevertheless, this data hardly accords with the indications that a group of businesspeople have amassed very substantial assets through a vigorous drive to acquire shareholdings in large companies. If they were to realise these assets they would have substantial funds in their bank accounts. On the other hand, white capital has always held a dominant position in the economy – in the 1980s six corporations controlled 70 per cent of the total assets of non-state corporations, and this has changed little. However, these same corporations now have an external reach that was not possible under apartheid. Five major corporations – Billiton, South African Breweries, Anglo American, Old Mutual and Dimension Data – have moved their primary listings from Johannesburg to the London Stock Exchange. This has rendered their domestic assets now wholly or partly-owned subsidiaries of foreign companies (Southall, 2005:460).

The case against the emergence of a strong black business class within the present system is that the economic legacy of colonial capitalism, rooted internally, remains in place. This system enabled white capital to gain enormous wealth and power through the extra-economic super-exploitation of forced cheap labour. Although the forced aspect of the system has gone, it remains extremely difficult to transform this system, and the economic and social dualism of the past remains structurally intact. Black business is operating within these structures and clearly benefits from the inherited capital–labour distortions.

One of the inescapable consequences is that black managers are paid the same financial rewards as their white counterparts, and sometimes a premium above the market rate, thereby expanding the size of the highly privileged bourgeoisie considerably. They are clearly part of the bourgeoisie by virtue of their location in the system of ownership and control of the means of production and by their incomes and lifestyle. They are therefore indirect beneficiaries of the economic dimensions of the apartheid legacy.

We have used the term 'class' with some reservations. Classes are large groups of people distinguished by their location in a system of social production, and by their relation to the means of production. The evidence suggests that black business is still too small a group to be a class-in-itself or a class-for-itself, despite vigorous aspirations. President Mbeki has actually criticised them for having become nothing more than *rentier* capitalists (Southall, 2003:12).

Some argue that the present process is intrinsic to capitalism. On the other hand, others believe that it may be possible to continue with deracialising the economy without the creation of an affluent black business class distinguished by conspicuous consumption and wealth accumulation through non-productive means. Some measures suggested are the prevention of the abuse of state procurement, control of offloading shares in state enterprises, limits on funding by the National Empowerment Fund, a requirement of commitments to social investment, and so on.

Black business has three options: (1) it can continue its strong linkages with the ANC and identify with its social and economic programme, which has a strong redistribution dimension; (2) it can strive to establish itself as a relatively independent force within the capitalist economy, resonant with traditional Marxist views of a progressive national bourgeoisie; or (3) it can become a junior partner of white capital, including its international dimensions. There are possibilities of some overlap of these options.

Much depends on how black business sees its own role. Many articulate an entitlement ideology demanding the same opportunities as white capital: 'If the whites can do it, so can blacks.' But this totally ignores the fact that white capital was based on super-exploitation and national oppression; mimicking their status deprives the black bourgeoisie of legitimacy and any scope for a progressive role.

Although the private sector is large in South Africa, seemingly offering ample scope for entry by a dynamic group of black entrepreneurs, the leap to capitalist status is not easy. Most start by deal-making to get a foot on the ladder of wealth accumulation. They are assisted by the openings offered by white business and by the BEE policies of the state. The latter is becoming an increasingly powerful weapon, as many large firms fear that those who do not make the necessary transition to empowerment may endanger their own sustainability. They fear that they will not get their customary share of government procurement, and that even the private banks may decline lending. 'Banks and other institutions will need to consider the risk of non-repayment when borrowers are not empowered' (*Business Day* Survey, May 2005).

A special report in *Time* magazine, 'The New Rand Lords: Capitalists or Cronies?', states that there are now 100 000 whites earning $60 000 annually, but only 5 000 blacks (*Time*, 6 June 2005). However, in the past three years 300 000 blacks became middle-income earners (between $13 000 and $23 000 annually). This is because blacks have been promoted vigorously in state institutions and because private companies must be seen to comply with training blacks and appointing them to management positions if they wish to benefit from government contracts. According to *Time*, 'the biggest companies offered to sell or grant equity stakes on favourable terms, often financed by the companies themselves, in return for connections, expertise and links to the black marketplace.' However some of the new black businesspeople assert that 'none of the new black elite control any independent capital'. The problem with this strategy is that most of the individuals involved land up in heavy debt since they have no capital to enter into these deals. Also, some become non-executive directors in order to collect fees but have no real power to influence the companies, as they are excluded from the inner circle running the companies.

However, notwithstanding the obstacles to capital accumulation, the mindset of enrichment and profit-making is growing rapidly as President Mbeki said. Even in the parastatal system, profit is sometimes primary. Telkom CEO Sizwe Nxasana was perhaps more brazen than most when he said, 'We are not apologetic about our profits, I'm in the business of making money; after all, we live in a capitalist society ... It used to be acceptable that the white population made money. Are you now suggesting that black companies should be socialist while the rest of the world is capitalist?'

In the present mood, where making money is a good thing, many political personalities with impeccable political credentials have moved into the private sector, followed by top public servants. They naturally retain their former political and family connections and clearly benefit from these associations in their new business roles (for details, see Southall, 2005:475). Southall comments: 'The point about these connections is not that they indicate corruption. However, what they do suggest is the fluidity, overlapping and intimacy of South Africa's black elite, which is still relatively small, amongst whom linkages across political, state and business boundaries provide a constant flow of exchanges and illuminate a sense of community' (Southall, 2005:476).

Whether this constitutes a basis for the emergence of 'crony capitalism' is still a subject for speculation. Certainly there are many instances of the use of opportunities provided by the state for accumulation in the private sector. The more important issue is whether the emergent business class is capable of becoming a dynamic productive capitalist class or whether it will be more akin to the state-dependent and kleptocratic class of post-independence Africa, driven more by conspicuous consumption than by a culture of hard work and productive effort. President Mbeki recently warned that 'independent Africa has provided some of the worst global examples of the gross abuse of state power to enrich elites that control the levers of state power' (speech in Parliament, 25 May 2005).

The ANC's liberation strategy was based on an intersection of race and class forces, which meant a combination of nationalist and class forces. It was argued that the working class was the most organised and determined, and with the most to gain, and was therefore the leading force. COSATU now argues that the working class has lost representation in the decision-making institutions of the ANC and has therefore lost much space to remain the leading force in the movement.

Furthermore, the economy has remained capitalist, with some of the main features of the past, namely, the dual economy and huge inherited inequalities. Many sections of the employed have improved their conditions, and the social wage has increased substantially, but class contradictions and exploitation continue despite the removal of repressive labour legislation.

The dual economy structure is typical of colonial and post-colonial societies. In the 'second economy' we find the poorest of the poor and marginalised people of such societies. Some of the workers in the formal economy are also among the poor.

However, to get a more balanced perspective, we have to compare the tasks facing the ANC during the struggle years to the many conflicting responsibilities facing it now: (1) it has to govern a very diverse society, sustain a growing economy and maintain social stability and cohesion; (2) it has to advance the interests of its primary constituency, the historically oppressed, especially the black masses and Africans in particular, and ensure the empowerment of women; (3) it has to ensure the advancement of the interests of the working class as well as the marginalised people on the periphery of the formal economy; (4) it has a long commitment to support Africa's renaissance, to oppose imperialist hegemony and advance the cause of progressive forces worldwide. A recent document states that 'the ANC should aim to contribute to the restructuring of international relations in the interests of the poor' (Preface to Strategy and Tactics, December 2002:25).

The motive forces
The complexity of these tasks has led to a debate about the nature

of the motive forces in the present period. This debate must be seen in the context of how the ANC sees the character of the national democratic revolution (NDR): 'The strategic objective of the NDR is the creation of a united, non-racial, non-sexist and democratic society. This, in essence, means the liberation of Africans in particular and Black people in general from political and economic bondage' (Strategy and Tactics, December 2002:30). It also refers to the 'elimination of apartheid property relations', 'the deracialisation of ownership and control of wealth, including land' and 'the elimination of the legacy of apartheid super-exploitation and inequality, and the redistribution of wealth and income to benefit society as a whole, especially the poor' (Strategy and Tactics, December 2002:24).

To advance these objectives, the ANC has identified the motive forces as follows: 'the black masses, those classes and strata that objectively and systematically stand to gain from the victory and consolidation of the NDR. It identifies the working class and the poor – in both rural and urban areas – as the core of these forces … These motive forces include the black, emergent capitalist class whose interests are served not only by the formal democracy, but also by the programme to change apartheid property relations … At the same time, the ANC needs to win over … all other sections of South African society, including the white workers, the middle strata and the bourgeoisie' (Strategy and Tactics, December 2002:25).

At the same time, it is acknowledged that these measures 'will not eliminate the basic contradiction between capital and labour … nor eradicate the disparate and sometimes contradictory interests that some of the motive forces of the NDR pursue. These secondary contradictions … must be properly managed' (Strategy and Tactics, December 2002:31). (The word 'secondary' may be challenged.)

Finally, there is a stark warning about the new social forces: 'the rising black bourgeoisie and middle strata are objectively important motive forces of transformation whose interests coincide with at least the immediate interests of the majority. But some are dictated to by foreign or local big capital on whom they rely for their advancement … without vigilance, elements of these new capitalist classes can become witting or unwitting tools of monopoly interests, or parasites who thrive on corruption in public office … Examples abound in many former colonies of massive disparities in the distribution of wealth and income between the new elite and the mass of the people … In South Africa this potential danger [resides] … With a coterie of mainly black men co-opted into the courtyard of privilege' (Strategy and Tactics, December 2002:33).

This implies that we must distinguish between the primary motive forces, their social base, the expected allies, the neutralised forces and the enemy forces. The motive forces therefore consist of:

- The black masses, especially the Africans
- The working class and the marginalised
- Progressive whites and other forces who identify with the ANC and accept the Freedom Charter
- The black middle strata
- Black officials in state institutions
- Black corporate managers in parastatals who identify with the Freedom Charter
- Elements of the emergent black capitalist class who identify with the ANC and the Freedom Charter despite their location in the institutions of exploitation.

Perhaps the most elusive category at present is the black middle class. Many are located in the state apparatus and are steadily moving up the ladder, with much blurring at the edges. Southall (2005) states that 29 per cent of the middle class was African in 1994, while the figure for 2000 was around 50 per cent. By

2005 the figure must be much higher. This category may be the primary beneficiaries of ANC rule.

Black personnel are now predominant throughout the top levels of the state system. This is most pronounced in government departments, with black women now also moving into top posts. But it is also highly visible in the parastatal system, which is now mostly in black control: this includes six of the nine directors of the Industrial Development Corporation (IDC); 12 of 23 directors of arms manufacturer Denel; 11 out of 15 directors of Eskom Holdings; and 9 out of 12 directors of Eskom. The same goes for Transnet, Telkom and South African Airways (SAA). The 15 state-owned enterprises deployed assets of R291 billion in 2003. If we add the R450 billion managed by the Public Investment Corporation (PIC), this constitutes a massive presence in the economy. Interestingly, many of these directors have positions on the boards of private companies, creating an intricate web of cross-influence (Southall, 2005:462).

However, a recent survey showed that black business has yet to enter the arena of manufacturing. There were 24 transactions in resources worth 58.3 per cent of the total deal, while in manufacturing there were 13 deals worth 1.3 per cent of the total deal. In basic industries, there were two deals worth zero of the total (Ernst & Young, 2004).

The key issue is whether the black business class is capable of playing the kind of role that similar groups have played in other developing countries. This includes promoting an economic strategy that boosts internal demand, promotes domestic industrial capacity and combines employment growth with redistribution (Southall, 2005c). There are few indications that South Africa's black business class has lined up behind such policies.

To conclude, we return to a comparison of the role of the domestic bourgeoisie in post-independence Africa and the situation in post-apartheid South Africa. In both cases, a sizeable local bourgeois class emerged within a decade of liberation. However, in the rest of Africa, this class was a creation of departing colonial powers, who sought to maintain their economic power by indirect means in a system of neocolonialism. In other words they were intrinsically comprador and parasitic. By contrast, in South Africa apartheid resisted the emergence of a black bourgeoisie till the very end. Hence, apart from some artificial measures in the Bantustans, no comprador class was in existence in 1994.

This is a vital difference, one which enabled the ANC to mobilise across a broad front of actual and aspirant classes-in-potential and maintain unity of the oppressed. This was one of the major consequences of a system of internal colonialism compared to the more usual colonial rule.

But the situation is changing rapidly. Now that the mechanisms of internal colonialism have been broken by the removal of white political rule, the abolition of the pass laws as well as the many laws of discrimination, a more 'normal' capitalist system is emerging, with all the contradictions of class becoming visible. However this 'normal' capitalism still faces a social structure rooted in the previous system of colonialism and underdevelopment. Our remedial measures are unlikely to be similar to those of developed 'normal' capitalism. Can the ANC government regulate our capitalism so that all benefit? Will the ANC be able to 'manage' the system so that we remove the obscene inequalities, poverty and joblessness that are still so pervasive?

President Mbeki's warning about the consequences of things falling apart is highly relevant.

Sources

African National Congress (2005). Strategy and Tactics. National General Council Resource Pack, Volume One, 29 June–3 July 2005.

Burger, R. & S. van der Berg (2004). 'Emergent black affluence and social mobility in post-apartheid South Africa'. Cape Town: Development Policy Research Unit, University of Cape Town.

Ernst & Young (2004). Data supplied in answer to Parliamentary Question no. 951.

Hirsch, Alan (2004). 'Overcoming underdevelopment in South Africa's second economy'. Conference paper, Pretoria, November 2004.

New Agenda (2006). Nos 21 and 22.

Southall, Roger (2004). 'The ANC and black capitalism in South Africa', in *Review of African Political Economy*, 100:313–28.

Southall, Roger (2005a). 'Black empowerment and corporate capital', in J. Daniel, R. Southall & J. Lutchman, *State of the Nation, South Africa 2004–5*. Cape Town: HSRC Press.

Southall, Roger (2005b). 'Political change and the black middle class in democratic South Africa'. Mimeo.

Southall, Roger (2005c). 'Can South Africa be a developmental state'. Mimeo.

Turok, Ben (2005a). 'Promoting production in the second economy', in *New Agenda: South African Journal of Social and Economic Policy*, Issue 18.

Turok, Ben (2005b). 'The Congress of the People, 1955', in *New Agenda: South African Journal of Social and Economic Policy*, Issue 18.

Turok, Ben (1999). 'Beyond the miracle. Development and economy in South Africa'. University of Western Cape.

Turok, Ben (1993). 'Development and reconstruction in South Africa'. Institute for African Alternatives, South Africa.

Part Three

The Global Environment

Chapter 14

Neoliberalism and Globalisation

During the 1960s, telecommunication technology made huge advances; engineers and communications experts began to invent new ways of interacting in all fields. Suddenly there was an understanding that, because of new technology, we were living in a global village.

After the Second World War, there was a move towards progressive government in many countries. In the United Kingdom, for example, the Labour Party came to power in 1945 and introduced the welfare state. However, as economic instability hit during the 1970s, there was a backlash against progressive policies and laws, in particular the welfare state and income redistribution. At the same time, there was a massive increase in capital mobility. In Lenin's writings on imperialism, he talked about industrial capital and financial capital. Starting in the 1970s, financial capital began to move around the world very fast, aided by computer technology. Indeed, money moved so fast that no one could keep track of it. In seconds, millions of dollars could move from Washington to Japan to China. Advances in telecommunications have enabled finance capital to move so fast around the world that the International Monetary Fund (IMF) has great difficulty in measuring the flow of finance across the world financial system. We live in a world where we do not really know what is happening.

Between 1986 and 1994, the so-called Uruguay Round of trade negotiations took place, and led to the establishment of the World Trade Organization (WTO). The first discussions were about free trade – abolishing protectionism, removing duties and tariffs and promoting free trade across the world. This occurred because the developed countries had surplus products and wanted to penetrate new markets, so they pushed for increased trade liberalisation for their own purposes. However, the stimulus to trade liberalisation also extended to industrial issues. Today we see the WTO discussing trade and investment, as well as issues around intellectual property. In the Uruguay Round of negotiations, the push was for free trade and free industrial penetration. By 2000, this kind of globalisation was widely accepted. It seemed so strong – globalisation of finance, free trade and industrial penetration – that everybody began to say that globalisation was here to stay.

Even in South Africa, Alec Erwin, the Minister of Trade and Industry at the time, was constantly telling us that globalisation offered challenges and opportunities as well as threats. Parliamentarians were consistently bombarded with the statement that globalisation was here to stay and offered huge advantages, and South Africa must become competitive. We were told that we had no choice in the matter, and that to resist free markets globally would be very dangerous. It was not only government that held this view; I am afraid the ANC also promoted it and put forward the argument that resisting globalisation would damage the country's chances to grow.

By 2000, there was widespread belief that globalisation – and the neoliberalism that accompanied it – was irresistible and unstoppable. Any country or government that tried to resist, or put obstacles in the way of globalisation, would be penalised. We were also told that government must retreat before market forces. We were told that we must reduce the size of the state. The Minister of Finance said this, the World Bank said this, the WTO said this, and all of our trading partners said that the South African state was too big and too strong and that we must allow the market to intervene. This was the view in 2000 in South

Africa and, I would say, almost around the world.

The East Asian countries and China were the exception to this rule. The East Asian countries – namely, South Korea, Malaysia, Taiwan and even Japan – refused to accept that globalisation was a good thing. All of these countries pursued their own route to development, and did not accept the argument for globalisation. In fact, they even put in place certain obstacles to free market access. For instance, South Korea imposed various duties, controls and tariffs in situations where they felt that the free market was going to undermine their economy. Frankly, these countries proved that you can resist the free market and globalisation and that you do not have to go the path of liberalisation.

Neoliberalism is an ideology. It emerged as a critique of the ideas of John Maynard Keynes, who was the greatest economist of the 20th century. Keynes was active in the 1930s and developed a huge body of knowledge about the functioning of capital markets and the market economy. I am not going to try and summarise his position here, but broadly it was very sceptical of the role of market forces in the economy. Keynes said that state intervention is important, and the key phrase that he introduced, still used today, is 'market failure'. Markets can fail. Neoliberalism argues that if you remove the obstacles to markets, this will ensure growth. Among these obstacles are tariffs, state investments, state interference, state regulation, and so on. Neoliberalism was only partly applied in the advanced countries, but the ideology was accepted. Neoliberalism flourished everywhere, just like globalisation, but in fact most governments did not implement neoliberalism fully. The reason for this is that in all the advanced countries the trade unions offered massive resistance, and civil society and parliaments all argued that if the ideology of neoliberalism was pushed too far, it would undermine the welfare state and the living standards of the people.

In the North they preached neoliberalism but did not implement it fully because the state, labour and civil society were strong and resisted the dismantling of health insurance, free education and so on. In the South they succeeded because the IMF and World Bank were so powerful, particularly in Africa and Latin America. These forces argued for a minimal state in Africa, a line we swallowed in 1995. Alec Erwin used to tell our committee that we needed a lean and mean state, and so budgets were cut, staffing levels were cut, staff employment was cut – all in the interests of a neoliberal approach to the state. We were told repeatedly that because of globalisation and international competition the South African economy must become competitive. Even as recently as late 2009, we heard some experts tell us that the South African economy must be competitive. If you want to be competitive then you have to impose all kinds of economic policies, including keeping labour costs down.

In the South, in Latin America and Africa, the neoliberal agenda ignored social and political pressures. Frankly, in countries like Ghana, Kenya and Nigeria, the trade unions are weak and they were unable to resist this push for a minimal state and for the reduction of welfare spending. In Zimbabwe, after independence, Robert Mugabe introduced free education and free health care. In the rural areas of Zimbabwe, the peasants were able to attend school free and go to free clinics. After a number of years, Mugabe was forced to adopt an IMF-imposed structural adjustment programme, and in no time the principle of cost recovery was imposed on the people of Zimbabwe. The rural people stopped going to school and going to clinics because of cost recovery: if you want to go to school you must pay; if you want to go to a clinic you must pay. This was the neoliberal agenda, which argued that in order to be competitive labour must work hard. The social and political pressures were disregarded.

In Latin America and Africa, the result of this neoliberal

agenda was that the welfare state was reduced and people began to suffer quite seriously as a result. The principle of social justice, which had been accepted throughout Africa at independence, was ignored. What mattered were profits, efficiency, competitiveness and market forces.

We can see that neoliberalism is still quite a strong force. But in the South (Latin America, Africa and Asia) we are beginning to say that we need more policy space. We accept globalisation, we understand that competitiveness is an important element, but we need to observe a certain prudence and caution in the way the state operates. You cannot just print money and spend recklessly, but you need to have policy space. When he was Minister of Finance, Trevor Manuel always said that because we were prudent in our finances we now have more policy space. The fact of the matter is that South Africa is not the United States. The policies that the US pursues are good for them or not so good for them, but they are not necessarily good for us. You cannot have one policy for the whole world. We all need to do our own mental work, understand where we are and develop our own policies. People in Africa and Latin America need to think about what works for them, and we need state intervention.

The developmental state is not part of neoliberalism. Neoliberals do not want to hear about a developmental state; they want a state to do anything except regulate laws. But we believe, as the ANC, that we need a developmental state, a state that is going to intervene in the economy and regulate imports and exports, and so on, because we have learned that there is such a thing as market failure. If you want to develop the rural areas, go and see what the private sector does there – that is market failure. Firstly, there is not enough demand for goods, so there is not enough money, there is no industry and there is no development in the rural areas and former homelands. There is market failure. The market does not do the job in those areas. The market may function and do its job in urban areas, particularly in industry, commerce and banking, but when you come to infrastructure there is market failure and the market does not do the job. This is the experience all over the Third World, whereas in the developed countries the market performs quite a strong role.

In East Asia the governments ignored the advice of neoliberals; they were pragmatic, and they developed a strong state. The South Korean state was in fact an authoritarian military state – they smashed the unions but they did develop the country. They created infant industries. In South Africa we do not create infant industries, and we have not done so for ten years because of the argument that infant industries are not competitive. Under the Zuma administration, with people like Ebrahim Patel and Rob Davies in key positions, perhaps we will begin to look at infant industries.

In South Korea they created industries by giving incentives. The government offered incentives (and subsidies) to manufacturers to produce specific products. For five years the motor car manufacturers in South Korea were losing money and so government subsidised production. After that five years they had developed the technology and capacity, and now South Korea exports motor cars all over the world.

About three years ago I visited China. I met a chief economist there who took me to a factory where they manufacture women's fashion – the fanciest clothing for the shops in Paris. When I asked about this, I learnt that in many industries they have signed partnership agreements. So, for example, this French company sends them their best designers, quality controllers and so on, and they teach the Chinese how to do it. The factories are Chinese but the designers and experts are French – initially, at least. Many industries in China are not Chinese in origin: Japan exported nearly all its major manufacturing industries to China; even Taiwan has built factories in mainland China because labour is cheap and because of China's huge market. It can be quite beneficial for a foreign company to go to China, establish a factory, install the machinery, send in the experts and then begin to manufacture with Chinese labour. The Chinese informed me that what used to happen in East Asia was often last-stage assembling manufacture. This is similar to the situation with our motor industry in South Africa; the engines and other components come from Germany and are assembled here. We do not own the technology.

The Chinese have adopted a different model. They said to foreign countries like France: you can come to our country on certain conditions, that you use our labour and resources and you teach our people, and after so many years we will not need you anymore. In this way China has absorbed the technology it lacked. We do not employ this strategy, and perhaps it is time we did so.

Another issue is local inputs. South Africa imports much of the raw materials we need for industry. For example, we used to import a lot of textiles for the garment industry. The South Koreans and the Chinese use local inputs, local infrastructure and local investment, and they use state-owned enterprises to feed into their own manufacture. South Africa has the cheapest electricity in the world, which is a wonderful asset. Frankly, if Eskom does not make a profit, it does not matter so much because that electricity is going into industries that boost our economy. We do not say to a hospital or a school, 'you must make profits'; so to the state-owned enterprises we must say: 'Do not be reckless but profit is not the main concern.' If you want to build industry, you must feed into that industry. We used to own Iscor, which produced cheap steel. Now our factories have to buy expensive steel, which pushes up the costs of the product in South Africa, and we become less and less competitive both internationally and within the domestic market.

Neoliberalism has taught the world that you must import. If you import cheap clothes, it is good for the consumer. But when you and I go to a shop and buy cheap Chinese clothing, we cut the jobs in our clothing industry and clothing workers get sacked. We have more or less shut down our textile and clothing industry because of imports. Our shoe industry is gone because of imports. So we face a choice as a country – do we keep goods or jobs? It is a simple equation; you can't have both. If you manufacture locally, the goods may cost more but you will have jobs. If you import cheap goods, you are going to lose factories – as we have done – and then you have cheap goods.

What the UN economists are saying is that it is better to give somebody a wage in order to buy more expensive goods than not to give him a wage and give him cheap goods. I am simplifying their argument, but basically neoliberalism says open up free markets, buy the cheapest in the world, and this is good for the consumer. While this may be true, it is also true that consumers become unemployed because factories close down. As a government, as the ANC, we have to start making choices like that – cheap goods or jobs. You cannot have both. You can take any industry in South Africa and ask: has the free market philosophy built jobs, built industry, created a strong economy, or not? Our banking sector is strong, our financial sector is strong and our manufacturing sector is very weak.

The final point to consider is that the economy does not exist or operate in isolation. All economies are rooted in a social and a political environment; for instance, we have heard Finance Minister Pravin Gordhan talking about taxation and how he is going to adjust taxes. This is a political decision, not only an economic decision. The budget requires revenue, and so you tax, but how much you tax is a political and a social decision. We reduced taxation for workers, and so workers pay very low taxes. When we discuss economics it is not merely a technical matter, but also a social and a political issue. That is why we have focused on globalisation and neoliberalism; these are political issues and they involve choices. The key thing about neoliberalism, in our experience, is that it has erased many social benefits that people had access to. We, as the ANC, have to be clear about whether we are going to continue with policies that contain elements of neoliberalism and structural adjustment or move towards a developmental state with a different profile and a different agenda, and this requires some fairly tough choices.

Chapter 15

The Role of the IMF and the World Bank

Before we move on to the topic of the International Monetary Fund (IMF) and the World Bank, I want to contextualise this discussion in the South African transition. When we started moving towards democracy, there was enormous pressure from outside that the ANC should not destroy the country. I'm putting it crudely, but there was great anxiety. Here was this rich, developed country, run by the apartheid government, and now there is a revolution by these ANC people. Are they going to destroy everything? All sorts of international forces took an interest in South Africa. In the early 1990s, while I was in Johannesburg and head of the ANC Economic Policy Desk in Gauteng, the World Bank also had offices in Johannesburg and they used to come and see me to lobby, as did the IMF. They were very active and very keen that the policies of the ANC should be moderate and cautious.

Sometimes we are a bit critical of the concessions the ANC made during the transition – the 'sunset clauses' and so on – but at the time there was enormous international interest in this country. For example, in 1990, according to the *Financial Mail*, President FW de Klerk was directly involved in meetings with the IMF and World Bank. His visit to Washington coincided with the presence of many other delegates from Africa. President Bush was sympathetic and offered to help bring about democracy in South Africa. De Klerk's more telling requirement was for South Africa to regain access to IMF support facilities, which had been blocked by the US, so that it could repay its foreign debt and regain access to world capital markets. So the whole question of South Africa's debt and access to international markets was very high on the agenda, with the IMF and the World Bank playing a major role.

The fact of the matter is that during the period of our transition to democracy there was huge international pressure. I would remind you that Trevor Manuel was head of the Department of Economic Planning in Shell House at the time, with Tito Mboweni as his deputy. Those two were actually driving economic policy during the transition, and they were subjected to enormous pressure from Washington. I could tell you many personal stories of my experience of all this, but I just want to establish the point clearly.

What are the IMF and the World Bank? What are their origins? I have written quite a lot on this subject. When I was in exile, I spent many years analysing and teaching the story of the IMF and World Bank and I've published dozens of articles on these institutions. In those days, I was head of a research institute in London, and I was invited to meetings all over the world to discuss the role of the World Bank and the IMF because there was a lot of concern about what these two institutions do.

The decision to start the World Bank and IMF was taken in July 1944 at the United Nations Monetary and Financial Conference, held at Bretton Woods in the USA. The Second World War was still raging, and the major European countries were in serious financial trouble. The stated purposes of the IMF, according to its Articles of Agreement, are 'to promote international monetary cooperation, to facilitate the expansion of international trade, to promote exchange stability, to assist with a multilateral system of payments, to help to correct maladjustments in balance of payments, to shorten disequilibrium in the international balance of payments of members' (IMF, 1993). Governments that were in deficit or bankrupt had to be bailed out, and the IMF would be there to lend money to those governments on a very big scale. The World Bank, on the other hand, was focused on projects, as a development bank. The IMF's job was to lend money to governments. It is a bank, not a charity. When the IMF says they want to help South Africa, they come as a bank to lend to you, and you must repay. They operate on business principles. The IMF is governed by a large international board. The World Bank also has a board of governors, who are actually called shareholders.

The United States has 16 per cent of the votes on the IMF board, and thus has a veto on the decisions of the Fund. The board meets to discuss policies and loans, and so on. In the end, after the discussions, if the United States objects they will veto any grant, loan or any deal to any country at all. They very seldom use the veto; they don't have to because everybody knows there's no point in fighting this issue because they are going to be beaten.

At first, because of the war, these institutions were focused on Europe. Indeed the IMF and the World Bank were not concerned with Africa or other Third World countries at all. They existed solely for Europe – to bail them out, and they did. After a while, they began to extend their interest to the Third World – Africa, Latin America and Asia.

The key turning point came in 1973, when the Organization of Petroleum-Exporting Countries (OPEC) – a cartel formed in the 1960s – imposed a huge increase in the price of oil. So the oil-rich countries soon had a lot of cash. The IMF and the World Bank went to these and other countries – including African countries like Nigeria and countries in Latin America – and persuaded them to borrow from the major banks, particularly Citibank, to industrialise their economies. It was very tempting for a government with a surplus – due to the oil bonanza – to be able to borrow from banks. Third World countries borrowed heavily, partly because interest rates were very low at that time. Then something strange happened. The interest rates rose, and all these governments fell into heavy debt to service their loans.

What is the role of the IMF? In the Articles of Agreement, or constitution, of the IMF, there is a section called 'Surveillance', which states: 'The fund shall oversee the international monetary system to ensure its effective operation.' Article B says: 'The Fund shall exercise firm surveillance; each member shall provide the Fund with the information necessary for such surveillance.' The Fund is actually an official authority, and its job is surveillance. There is a clause under Article 4 of this constitution which empowers the Fund to go to any country and inspect its books. Every year, sometimes twice a year, the Fund comes to South Africa. The first thing they do is go and see the Reserve Bank. They may go and see the Treasury and ask to see the books. They look at all the financial data, and they issue a report. These reports used to be confidential and go to the board of directors of the Fund, who would decide if a country should be able to borrow or not. After a while there was a lot of international pressure, and so the Fund began to issue two reports: one is the public report for the media and the other is the confidential report for the board. A copy of the confidential report is given to the government.

I was a member of the Finance Committee for 10 years, and I tried for years to get hold of copies of that confidential report. I never succeeded. Parliament does not have access. It belongs to the Treasury and the Minister of Finance, and they wouldn't disclose it. What they did after a while was to disclose the public report, which was rather a press release on the IMF's findings about the South African economy. The public report is fairly tame and is meant not to embarrass anybody.

One of the reasons the IMF compiles these reports is that Third World countries are in debt. The debts used to be massive, and many countries in Africa have borrowed from the Fund. However, South Africa never borrowed. The one thing the ANC government has not done is borrow from the Fund, and there's a very good reason for that. The moment you borrow, they impose conditions. These include all sorts of requirements, such as the devaluation of your currency. I used to teach at the University of Zambia. When I arrived there, one pound sterling was worth about 6 kwacha. By the time I left, three years later, you were getting 15 or 20 kwacha because the devaluation of the currency was so fast. After I left, devaluation escalated and today almost everywhere in Africa one dollar is worth a thousand, two thousand or three thousand of the local currency. In other words, those currencies are not convertible on the international market – they are really just paper money.

Other conditions imposed by the IMF are curbs on imports and the removal of subsidies. Throughout Africa after independence, subsidies were introduced. If we take Zimbabwe as an example, in the beginning Robert Mugabe introduced subsidies for health and education. Children could go to school and clinics free because those services were subsidised by the state. Many countries in Africa did the same thing, like Zambia, where there were subsidies for all kinds for things. But then they were told that this is socialism and they must remove the subsidies and become cost-effective.

Then there is the removal of price controls. After independence, many countries in Africa introduced price controls, especially on food. Zimbabwe is a case in point. Mugabe did a good job at the beginning with price controls. Zambia had price controls on mealie meal, allowing the masses to buy things at a low price. The IMF said that was socialism and to get rid of it.

All governments that fell under IMF lending had to curb their spending. Government spending was cut; all services and infrastructure that the independent governments had put in place in the beginning were cut, and governments were told to reduce their expenditure.

Then, finally, economic liberalisation of all kinds was promoted. Countries had to open up their economies to foreign imports and goods. So those were some of the conditionalities imposed in Africa, Latin America and Asia on anyone who went to the IMF or World Bank for loans.

The conditions imposed by the IMF and World Bank are put together in a formula called a structural adjustment programme (SAP). The imposition of SAPs on almost all African governments led to several 'lost decades' of development. While the Bank placed all the blame for Africa's decline on its governments, the Organisation of African Unity (OAU) responded that the crisis and economic collapse were due to overwhelming external shocks: soaring interest rates, declining commodity prices, growing protectionism and growing debt service payments. 'Debt service payments for Africa rose from 15 per cent of export earnings in 1980 to 31 per cent in 1986' ... 'In real terms, resource transfers to Africa declined from $10 billion in 1982 to $1 billion in 1985' (Cheru, 1989:14).

Some economists showed that there was a real transfer of finance from Africa to the World Bank rather than the reverse. Between 1982 and 1990, total payments of interest and capital by the South were a staggering R3 725 billion. During the same period there was a flow of finance from North to South of R2 567 billion, leaving a net reverse flow to the North of R1 158 billion. During the same period, sub-Saharan debt increased by 113 per cent and Africa paid back R500 billion – its worst economic period in recent history (Turok, 1993:156). The Nigerian economist Bade Onimode has stated that, since the implementation of the structural adjustment programmes in the 1980s, the growth of GDP per head was minus 3.4 per cent for 1980–86; for exports, it was minus 1.9 per cent. Africa's total external debt was $55 billion in 1980, and rose to $85 billion in 1985 and $200 billion in 1987. Total external debt service payments rose from $465 million in 1970 to $8.5 billion in 1985, that is, from 5.4 per cent to 21.3 per cent in 1985 (Onimode, 1987). Onimode later added that 'The total net outflow from

South to North between 1985 and 1990 was $156 billion or $31 billion annually, while the net outflow to the World Bank and IMF was $1 billion annually' (Onimode, 1992:14).

To come back to South Africa, we made one agreement with the World Bank that I know of, but I'm afraid it was confidential. Alec Erwin gave me a copy in 1995–96 and told me it was 'for my eyes only'. I have kept it a secret and never shown it to anybody. It was a technical agreement with the Bank about skills development and technical advice. It was the only agreement at that time. We did not make an agreement with the Fund because we did not want to borrow. The moment you borrow, you fall into the trap of conditionalities. Since then, we have made other agreements with the Bank, and we do have quite a number of technical agreements. But I think on the whole those things are not offensive or difficult. They are technical agreements; they do research for us, give some advice and train some people. There was one agreement in 1994, under which about 30 people went to Washington for several months' training in macroeconomic policy. When they came back, you almost couldn't recognise them! They were all bankers and funders, and we were told this is the way to run the country. I'm afraid we swallowed that piece of poison. Some of them went to work in the National Treasury and they became fans of the IMF and the World Bank policies.

South Africa did not borrow from the IMF and World Bank, so we did not officially adopt an SAP, but instead we adopted the Growth Employment and Redistribution (GEAR) strategy (introduced in 1996). GEAR was actually written by a staff member of the World Bank who was seconded to National Treasury. On one occasion he came to the Finance Committee to present GEAR, and some of us were rather hostile. The trade union movement was wildly opposed, the Communist Party was hostile and there were lots of people in the ANC who were very unhappy about GEAR. When he finished his presentation, I asked him: 'Are you an employee of the World Bank?' I was trying to embarrass him, but he said: 'I'm a South African by birth.' I just wanted to show that GEAR had this very strong hand in the World Bank and indeed was crafted along the lines of an SAP. In fact, some of our responsible ministers actually said we've got a structural adjustment policy. It was indeed structural adjustment, but I don't want to go into detail about what it was and what it wasn't. The conditionalities became a cause for very serious concern.

What are the effects of these policies? Will Hutton, former editor of *The Observer* and a first-class economist, once asked if I would join a conference to set up what he called a 'shadow Bretton Woods system', an alternative to the international monetary system set up in 1944. I said of course, but it never happened. He said that the IMF has forced developing markets to open up to global capitalism. Those of us who know about the Economic Partnership Agreements (EPAs) and the World Trade Organization (WTO) know that what they're trying to do is to open up our markets and the whole of Africa to imports from the developed countries. This started during the 1980s when the IMF opened up an 'austere remedy for deflated economies, steep increases in interest rates, cuts in public spending'. This is important because frankly our ministers of finance, one after the other, talk about stabilisation, stable prices, stabilise the currency, stabilise the economy, and so on. Well, stabilisation in Africa has led to high levels of unemployment, increases in the cost of food and fuel and, in many countries, instability.

When I was teaching at the University of Zambia, the terms of Zambia's SAP forced President Kenneth Kaunda to deflate the economy, devalue the currency, cut government spending and increase food prices. As a result, miners in the Copperbelt went on strike. They rioted and people were shot and killed. We called those the 'IMF riots' because IMF pressure led Kaunda to do certain things which led to those riots.

People across Africa understand the consequences of the IMF

policies. I remember going to a conference in Nigeria with Rob Davies. We got into a taxi at Lagos airport and while driving into town I asked the taxi driver, a little provocatively, 'Do you know about the IMF?' He said 'SAP', of course. Rob was very surprised to see that this illiterate taxi driver knew all about SAPs. Then we went into a little shop where they was some lovely Nigerian cloth. Rob was rather interested in buying some of it and I asked the lady there in this little shop: 'Do you know of SAP?' She said: 'SAP, oh yes, debt! Nigeria has been killed by this.' Ordinary people in Nigeria, Ghana and Kenya knew of the SAP because of the consequences for employment. The conditionalities are what has killed Africa. These imposed the reduction of subsidies, benefits, welfare and state expenditure, budget and investment cuts and led to an increase in unemployment and devaluation of currencies. This is quite contentious; some people disagree, and there are many discussions about this. In 2006 the Norwegian government adopted a policy under which they would no longer provide funds for the World Bank in cases where conditionalities are imposed. This is not some radical voice, but a Western capitalist government.

The Norwegian decision emerged following a study entitled 'The World Bank and IMF's Use of Conditionality to Encourage Privatisation and Liberalisation: Current Issues and Practices'. The study records the actual negotiations between the Bank and Mozambique on an energy reform and access project, which began in 2000 with Norwegian involvement. Energy was meant to be an important factor in the Poverty Reduction Action Plan for Mozambique. The study states: 'This is a case that ... paints an intriguing picture of a dynamic process involving conditionalities, privatisation, bilateral and multilateral donors' (Norwegian Ministry of Foreign Affairs, 2006:36).

The study records the case of Uganda, where the 'main emphasis is the conditionality process in a budget support context, tied to a poverty reduction plan'. The next case is

Zambia, which 'provides insight into how the relationship between the government and the IMF has developed over time'. The Norwegian study concludes: 'The degree of coercion involved is difficult to determine, but the International Financial Institutions (IFIs) clearly espouse particular policy agendas which they promote.' They also note that 'for many African countries the 1980s and 1990s was a period of declining national sovereignty, compared with the 1960s and 1970s' (Norwegian Ministry of Foreign Affairs, 2006:46). The report advocates 'moving towards greater national sovereignty in aid dependent countries, while increasing accountability for results' (Norwegian Ministry of Foreign Affairs, 2006:47).

Sometimes the World Bank says they don't impose conditionalities, but when a country borrows from the World Bank, the World Bank has to get a certificate from the IMF. Without that certificate of approval, the loan is rejected. Although the World Bank will insist it is independent, in the end it is the IMF that controls the process.

The other thing is that the Fund and the Bank are sisters. Every year there is a conference of the Fund and the Bank. They meet formally and officially to hammer out policy. So the Bank can't say they are independent. They might be autonomous to a degree but their policies are set at these annual conferences and nothing moves unless there's agreement.

I have another document from the International Monetary Fund called the Public Information Notice, issued in 2005 after they concluded the Article 4 Consultation with South Africa. They used the word 'consultation'. In official documents they don't use the word 'surveillance' except in the constitution, as I indicated earlier. This was a consultation with South Africa held on 2 September 2005. They said the following: 'We encourage the authorities to consider reducing the scope of centralising collective bargaining.' Now, try telling NUMSA and the other unions that the IMF says you must reduce 'centralised collective bargaining'. They don't like unions; they want people to negotiate at local level. You can have a union on the shop floor, but not nationally. The other thing is 'simplifying' the minimum wage structure for farmworkers and for domestic workers and streamlining dismissal procedure.

In another report on a 'consultation' (IMF, 11 July 2007), it is stated that the 'Executive Directors commended the authorities for their well-designed macroeconomic policies and structural reforms ... Directors supported the authorities' strategy to deal with [unemployment and poverty] through policies aimed at raising economic growth while maintaining a stable macroeconomic environment.' The report contains detailed analysis and data on South Africa's economic performance that goes way beyond a normal financial report.

Let me quickly recap. In 1992–93 there was huge sensitivity about the democratic transition internationally – among investors, the IMF and World Bank and the rating agencies. Everybody outside was dead scared that the Communist-led ANC was going to take over and destroy the economy. They put enormous pressure on the ANC leadership to show respectability and exercise caution and forced the ANC into a very cautious macroeconomic policy. It was part of the deal at that time. I don't blame anybody for that.

Then in 1994 we had the RDP. I was head of the RDP in Gauteng and Jay Naidoo was the national minister. But after nine months Jay Naidoo was fired, I was fired and the RDP offices were closed down everywhere. Instead of that, we got GEAR, introduced primarily due to pressure from the World Bank.

In conclusion, in South Africa we have been careful. We have not borrowed from the IMF, but we have adopted policy that is friendly to structural adjustment. My own view is that we pay a price for that. Even though we are not in debt, we do listen to them and we are very careful.

Sources

Bull, Benedicte, Alf Morten Jerve & Erlend Sigvaldsen (2006). 'The World Bank's and IMF's use of Conditionality to Encourage Privatisation and Liberalisation'. Report prepared for the Norwegian Ministry of Foreign Affairs as background for the Oslo Conditionality Conference, November 2006. Available from http://www.duo.uio.no/sok/work.html?WORKID=66872; accessed 22 December 2010.

Cheru, Fantu (1989). *The silent revolution in Africa*. London: Zed Books.

International Monetary Fund (1997). Articles of Agreement. Available from http://www.imf.org/external/pubs/ft/aa/; accessed on 22 December 2010.

International Monetary Fund (1997). *Good governance: the IMF's role*. Available from http://www.imf.org/EXTERNAL/PUBS/FT/EXRP/GOVERN/govern.pdf; accessed 22 December 2010.

Onimode, Bade (1995). *Issues in African development*. Nigeria: Africa Centre for Development and Strategic Studies (ACDESS).

Onimode, Bade (1992). *A future for Africa*. London: Earthscan and Institute for African Alternatives (IFAA).

Onimode, Bade (ed.) (1987). The IMF, World Bank and Africa. Report on a Conference. London: Institute for African Alternatives (IFAA).

Structural Adjustment Participatory Review International Network (SAPRIN) (2004). *Structural adjustment: the SAPRI report*. London: Zed Books.

Turok, Ben (1993). 'Prey of the debt-mongers', in *Development and reconstruction*. London: Institute for African Alternatives (IFAA).

TWN Info Service, 2 October 2007.

Chapter 16

Policy Dimensions of Trade in the SADC Region

I have been asked to discuss the meaning and importance of 'developmental regionalism' for the states and people of southern Africa, and to indicate an appropriate role for policy-makers, parliamentarians and civil society in shaping this debate. This is quite a big task.

Before turning to policy issues, let me briefly present some data drawn from the 2007 IMF Report drawn up for the 2007 Article 4 Consultation. For Africa as a whole, South Africa accounts for over a third of sub-Saharan African GDP. Direct investment in other parts of Africa has doubled since 2000, amounting to R3.7 billion in 2004. Sixty of the top companies listed on the JSE have direct ownership of foreign affiliates in Africa, while another 26 are holding companies with investments in Africa. South African banks operate in 17 countries.

South Africa belongs to a Common Monetary Area (CMA) with Lesotho, Swaziland and Namibia; the Southern Africa Customs Union (SACU), consisting of the CMA states plus Botswana; and the 15-nation Southern African Development Community (SADC). South Africa accounts for two-thirds of the combined SADC GDP and for about 60 per cent of intra-SADC trade. A possible free-trade area is under discussion.

South Africa also has trade agreements with many other countries, notably the European Union (Trade, Development and Cooperation Agreement), the United States and China. The SACU is negotiating an Economic Partnership Agreement with the European Union (EU).

Since 1994, South Africa has pursued a policy of opening-up, with substantial lowering of tariffs in the pursuit of greater competitiveness. However, the country's share of exports in world markets is at the same level as in the late 1990s, with South Africa's market share falling throughout the period, according to data from the IMF.

These trends support the case for greater efforts in trade with the whole of Africa and the SADC region.

The policy arena

It can be seen that there has been a degree of regional integration in southern Africa for some time. However, developmental regionalism is an entirely different matter, going way beyond considerations of customs union, trade preferences and the like. In current debates, regionalism is seen in the context of a united Africa, based on political unity, economic cooperation and much else.

Allow me briefly to refer to some policy reference points that we all know, but which ought to be signalled here. The foundation for this approach was laid down by Adebayo Adedeji in the 1980 Lagos Plan of Action, which was endorsed by the Organisation of African Unity (OAU) and the United Nations (UN). The Lagos Plan was attacked in the World Bank's infamous Berg Report and then shelved. The Lagos Plan argued that Africa was 'over-dependent on the export of basic raw materials and minerals' and should instead 'promote the goals of rapid self-reliance and self-sustaining development and economic growth' in the pursuit of 'a far-reaching regional approach based primarily on collective self-reliance'. This would 'pave the way to an African Common Market leading to an African Economic Community' (OAU, 1980).

Adedeji persisted with his views when he was head of the UN Economic Commission for Africa (UNECA), but with little success. In the early 1990s, his concern shifted to the role of South Africa in Africa, displaying much scepticism about whether South Africa would play a significant role in identifying with the rest of the continent, rather than strengthening relations with Europe. He convened a conference in Windhoek in January 1994, and published the papers in a book entitled *South Africa and Africa, Within or Apart?* (1996).

The South African Parliament began considering this theme at a special committee established to consider the African Union (AU), and in particular the creation of the Pan-African Parliament (PAP). A research project was initiated to consider the particular features of developmental regionalism, as opposed to the orthodox model of customs union, free trade, etc. A research proposal submitted by the Africa Institute of South Africa (AISA) argued that the success of both the African Union and the New Partnership for Africa's Development (NEPAD) hinged on regional integration. The document urged the need for a conceptual road map and analysis of the content of regional economic communities (RECs) as integration models. Such analysis had to deal with diversifying the export base, harmonisation of currencies, harmonising industrial policy, encouraging complementarities and overcoming resistance to integration (AISA, 2002). In another submission, the Economic Policy Research Institute (EPRI) argued for a political-led integration that supports broader socio-economic development (EPRI, 31 July 2002). The question of political will was thus seen as a central issue. Unfortunately, neither proposal was pursued.

NEPAD introduced a strong emphasis on regional integration as the foundation for Africa's unity. It stated that 'NEPAD is a holistic, integrated sustainable development initiative for the economic and social revival of Africa' (Progress Report, July 2002, p. 2). 'The regional economic communities remain the building blocks for Africa's economic integration' (Action Plans, July 2002, p. 7). This approach has had much formal endorsement from multilateral agencies, but has led to little in concrete terms. In part this is because the developmental aspect of regionalism has often been displaced by more conventional criteria. A meeting of ministers of finance with the Commission for Africa in Cape Town in January 2005 stated: 'The potential for regional integration is largely unrealised. By removing African barriers to trade – in tariffs, trade facilitation, customs administration, sea and air regulation – accelerated regional integration can provide a springboard to creating more competitive industries on a global stage, and increasing growth.'

During many of these discussions, one theme stood out as a necessary dimension of developmental as opposed to formal regionalism, namely, the fact that right across Africa, state boundaries were artificial and often ignored by rural people, who traded as though these boundaries did not exist. There is evidence that even in the southern African region, there is a considerable amount of informal trading that bypasses customs posts. Clearly, developmental regionalism ought to take account of such linkages and build on them, even if they derogate from customs receipts.

Unfortunately, many officials do not share this view, and concentrate on the money they can glean from cross-border trade as a contribution to the national fiscus. My personal experience in Tanzania confirms this view. I proposed to the Zimbabwean, Kenyan and Zambian embassies that a publishing initiative be set up in which each of the four countries could join as both publishers of academic books and as a market. This would be highly beneficial, effectively creating a common market with no duties. I was told that the loss of duties was an obstacle, and Zimbabwe for instance preferred to import books from the UK at low tariffs, for reasons I could not discover.

Gabriel Oosthuizen has done an admirable job of setting out the broader dimensions of developmental regionalism, which go way beyond trade. But these proposals have yet to find their way into the wider arena of policy-making and public consciousness. Indeed, it may be that as long as the negotiators remain locked into financial considerations alone, the absence of a positive environment for regionalism could frustrate the whole project. He says: 'It is sometimes unclear whether a socio-economic co-operation treaty, the RISDP, its implementation framework, reflects current policies and strategies in a particular area of co-operation' (Oosthuizen, 2006:229).

What role for policy-makers?

Experience thus far with creating a favourable environment for developmental regionalism is that neither the AU nor its institutions are able to give adequate impetus for it to happen in a reasonable time-frame. In part this is due to the preponderance of national interests in decision-making, with the broader goals of African Unity and NEPAD not bearing the same weight as national concerns. Even a fairly active body like the Economic Community of West African States (ECOWAS) has not made major visible gains in the regional integration of economies. Policy-makers have to make far more deliberate efforts to ensure that a broad vision pervades all the discussions about regionalism. They have to go beyond the kind of formulations found in the protocol for the creation of a SADC Parliament, which refers to 'regional cooperation, self-reliance and economic efficiency' but gives little direction on a deeper form of regional integration (Protocol on the SADC Parliament, article 3.4, Maseru, 2003).

In his book *The Writing on the Wall: China and the West in the 21st Century*, economist Will Hutton argues persuasively that economic advance requires much more than investment and trade. It requires a favourable democratic environment, supportive public institutions and values, and 'soft infrastructure'. He stresses the importance of a 'network of democratic institutions constituting a public realm rather than just representative government' (Hutton, 2007:184).

His approach goes much further than the 'good governance' requirements of the donor institutions of the North, and poses a challenge to intellectuals and policy-makers when we consider the requirements of regional integration.

In short, our discussions should focus as much on the commitment of the relevant governments and our societies as on the more technical issues, such as physical infrastructure, trade barriers, investment, opportunities for business, constitutional and legal instruments and the like, important as they are (NEPAD Dialogue, 8 September 2006).

The stubborn clinging to sovereignty continues to be a major hurdle. 'Integration is constrained because countries guard their sovereignty, protocols take long to ratify and implement, and countries find it easier to liberalise the movement of people rather than goods and investment' (African Regional Integration Strategy workshop, World Bank, Nairobi, 31 January 2007).

There is also the problem of external interests. Foreign investors in Africa's minerals and other natural resources do not have the same motivation to create regional entities. This is confirmed by analysis of official development assistance (ODA), now a major contributor to many African country budgets. Research by the World Bank and other multilateral institutions has confirmed a tendency, revealed by a campaign on monitoring ODA led by the NEPAD Contact Group of African Parliamentarians and the Association of European Parliamentarians (AWEPA), for individual donor countries to be reluctant to share information and coordinate efforts which would diminish relations with their own 'patch'. In other words, they prefer country-to-country relations rather than region-to-region relations.

The Pan-African Parliament obviously has an important role to play, although it is constrained by a lack of finance and by tensions with the AU and the Commission. The PAP could also exert pressure on their governments finally to decide on which regional economic blocks each country will belong to.

African research institutions such as CODESRIA could help a great deal, if they would shake off their deep pessimism about the prospects of a more progressive Africa under its current leadership.

Africa's civil society organisations could also provide some momentum, if they too would engage more effectively in the public terrain occupied by governments and formal African institutions. When the AU and its structures do engage in consultations with civil society, they should resist official efforts to confine discussion to formal institutional arrangements at the expense of more fundamental political concerns (African Union–Civil Society Consultative Meeting, Abuja, 22 January 2005).

Concluding remarks

Momentum towards real integration through developmental regionalism as the foundation for Africa's unity will have to depend on more than technical negotiations for customs unions, free trade and the rest. It requires buy-in from many different sectors of society, for reasons that go beyond immediate national interest.

Intellectuals and activists can make a useful contribution in placing much greater emphasis on the social and political benefits of building the 'soft infrastructure' associated with 'public goods' and the 'public realm' as the sound foundation for developmental regionalism.

Perhaps the harsh conditions that the great powers continue to impose on Africa through EPAs and other instruments – which include farming subsidies, non-tariff barriers and other measures to exclude Africa's products – while demanding access to Africa's domestic markets will be enough to awaken the urge for more rapid progress for African unity.

Sources

Adedeji, Adebayo (1996). *South Africa and Africa: within or apart?* London: Zed Books.

African Institute of South Africa (AISA) (2002). Identification and analysis of economic integration strategies in Africa. Report submitted to Parliament, 2002.

Hutton, Will (2007). *The Writing on the wall: China and the West in the 21st century.* London: Little Brown & Company.

Organisation of African Unity (OAU) (1980). Lagos Plan of Action for the Economic Development of Africa.

Oosthuizen, Gabriel (2006). *The Southern African Development Community.* Institute for Global Dialogue.

Chapter 17

Africa and the Economic Partnership Agreements (EPAs)

Because the rules governing trade between Europe and Africa have become increasingly complex, we need to set down some basic issues. In colonial times, trade between the colonial powers and the colonies was marked by unequal exchange, with the values wholly out of proportion. In the period of European industrialisation, European manufacturing relied on protection behind high tariff walls, which kept out cheaper imports. In the present period of so-called free market economics, Europe continues to maintain massive protectionism while demanding opening-up by trading partners. Europe wants access for manufactured goods and services in Africa, which will seriously weaken the domestic economy.

All these negotiations are conducted in highly complex terms, and in numerous extended sessions, possibly designed to obscure Europe's real intentions. Where small concessions are given by Europe, they are immediately compensated for by additional demands. If we are moving to a system of global free markets, why not make a few simple rules, which will apply to all, without any complexity, and without any hidden advantages to the strong?

Failed negotiations at the WTO
The establishment of the World Trade Organization (WTO) was meant to usher in a global system of rule-based free trade from which all would benefit. The underlying theory was that countries would benefit from liberalising their imports and

exports, by virtue of greater access to each other's markets. The theory ignores the experience of the developed countries, which used protectionism behind which they industrialised until they were strong enough to compete with others (Chang, 2002).

The WTO has failed to reach agreement, even though the Doha Development Round was supposed to be based on fostering development in Africa and other developing countries. Indeed all the negotiations have been marked by massive resistance to giving significant concessions by the developed world.

Even in the present period, the developed countries, notably the US, EU and Japan, maintain high protectionist walls around their agriculture, in addition to massive financial support to farmers. This makes them hugely advantaged over African agricultural exports.

In addition, the developed countries wish to include new issues in world agreements – the so-called Singapore 'new generation' issues – such as investment agreements with rights of establishment, competition, intellectual property and government procurement (Davies, 2008). The effect of this would be the undermining of Africa's service industries, local procurement advantages and the loss of much intellectual property.

The importance of multilateralism

Despite these difficulties, developing countries continue to argue for a rule-based multilateral system of trade, since it enables poor countries to build a united front in negotiations. Long experience shows that where there is a bilateral system, the rich country will always be stronger than the poor partner and inevitably take advantage. Indeed, even in international politics, the world is moving to multilateral arrangements, as in the UN system, rather than bilateral negotiations.

Dot Keet, an expert on the Lomé and Cotonou agreements, argues that from the late 1990s, the European Commission

(EC) in Brussels began putting ever-greater pressure on the 79 African, Caribbean and Pacific (ACP) governments to accept that they could no longer continue to have preferential trade terms with Europe, and that the Lomé Convention would have to be replaced. Faced with continued pleas and protests from the ACP governments, the EC assured them that they would continue to receive financial and technical aid and that their future relations with the European Union (EU) would be located within new 'economic partnership' agreements (EPAs).

The EC argued that the Lomé trade regime of preferential trade arrangements was not compliant with WTO rules because it was non-reciprocal and therefore open to challenge in the WTO. It was replaced by the Cotonou Agreement in 2000. The EC assured these countries of continuing 'aid' and 'partnership' in future relationships. However, despite assurances that the ACP countries would not be worse off, there were indications that they would have reduced preferences, and that in return for access to EU markets, they would have to reduce their own tariffs and open up to EU exporters, i.e.'reciprocation' (Keet, 2008).

The principle of 'reciprocation', as between a strong trading partner and a weak one, can only be fair if it is based on 'asymmetry', that is, the strong giving more concessions than the weak. So how is this addressed in the EPAs?

What is an Economic Partnership Agreement (EPA)?

The documentation on trade relations has always been very complex. This has been a great handicap for African negotiators, who do not have the same expert backup as the Europeans and cannot afford the huge staff and other costs. The EPA negotiations are burdened with the same complexity, although African negotiators are now more experienced and united than before.

An EPA is a preferential trade agreement that aims at reducing and substantially eliminating barriers to free trade, such as tariff and non-tariff barriers. Free trade agreements are made possible by Article XXIV of the General Agreement on Tariffs and Trade (GATT). EPAs were set to be in place by 1 January 2008.

The EPA negotiating partners consist of the EU and the ACP group of countries. The EPAs are supposed to address trade imbalances between the EU and ACP by offering the Least Developed Countries (LDCs) and other countries of the ACP an opportunity to grow their economies by tapping into the larger EU market.

The EPAs have taken shape on a bilateral basis. However, the EU itself now favours regional agreements with the ACP countries because it will be very much easier and 'more efficient' for the EC to negotiate with groups of ACP countries, rather than with dozens of them individually. It would also be more worthwhile and more profitable for EU investors and producers/ exporters to operate in future in the larger combined markets of such countries, or take on huge infrastructure projects created between groups of such countries, and so on.

The EPAs have taken place against the backdrop of much broader negotiations at the WTO to produce a developmental outcome, with much emphasis on agriculture. However, developing countries are faced with demands for concessions, especially in the area of industrial goods, where developing countries seek to protect their sensitive products from the effect of lower tariffs. At the same time, rich countries are averse to reducing subsidies for their local producers, as this may negatively affect the competitiveness of their exports. Trade in services is another contentious issue in the talks, as many developing countries' economies are not strong enough to compete with rich countries in the services sector. Nevertheless, an agreement on agriculture will be an important developmental outcome, as this is one of the critical sectors for developing countries – if not the most important.

Who gains, who loses?

While the fundamental aim of the EPAs is that developing countries open their markets to EU manufactured goods and agricultural exports, there is also a hidden agenda of opening up to European investors, to European services companies, to government procurement contracts and other services. It should be remembered that in the present world economy, the services sector – information services in particular – is expanding much faster than manufacturing, and that countries like India have developed a comparative advantage over Europe in this area.

Serious challenges therefore remain, as developing countries have to contemplate concessions, especially in the area of industrial goods. Developing countries should seek to protect their sensitive products from the effect of lower tariffs on their side and subsidies given by developed states to their local producers.

The urge to penetrate developing-country markets is now overwhelming. In some industries in Europe there is excess capacity, and they want to offload goods in Africa. They also want to take over banking and insurance from local enterprises, including government-owned enterprises, thereby further eroding the economic independence of African countries.

The essential point is that at Doha there was consensus that it was vital for poor countries to be allowed to develop and not be hindered by barriers of any kind. Unfortunately, the world trade system shows no sign of allowing this to happen.

A conference in Berlin on 9–10 March 2006, organised by the German Institute for International and Security Affairs, focused on the proliferation of free trade agreements, of which there were 300. The main reason for the proliferation, especially in South-East Asia, was the slow progress in WTO negotiations. The agreements have also weakened existing regional organisations for economic integration, such as APEC and ASEAN.

The emphasis on bilaterals was diverting scarce resources

away from the WTO negotiations. But bilateral agreements always favour the strong. They also lack transparency. Even the bilaterals between Australia and the US have brought disadvantage to the former, partly because of the complex rules of origin often used as protectionist devices. Only goods produced within a free trade area qualify for duty-free trade. They have also not brought a significant contribution to the liberalisation of trade. Dr Heribert Diter, of the Warwick Commission on International Financial Reform, concluded: 'The country's credibility in trade negotiations is weakened, its sovereignty reduced, and the potential for Australian companies to integrate themselves in international production networks weakened.'

Case studies: SADC (**Southern Africa Development Community**) and SACU (**South African Customs Union**)

South Africa signed a bilateral trade agreement in the form of the Trade, Development and Cooperation Agreement (TDCA) with the EC, and renewed this in November 2007. It believed that it had no choice as South Africa has special needs with respect to its largest trading partner. South Africa did not qualify for the special preferential market access under the Cotonou system because of the huge size of its economy and its level of development. However, many difficulties have arisen, as indicated below.

Having a separate agreement with the EU has had the unintended effect of causing trade imbalances and revenue losses for other members of SACU. This has ultimately had the effect of undermining regional integration instead of promoting it – one of the basic premises of the EPAs.

Furthermore, South Africa, as the coordinator of the SADC negotiating group, refused in November 2007 to sign EPAs with the EU. Although SADC has 14 member states, only 7 were part of the SADC EPA configuration.

According to Rob Davies, at the time Deputy Minister of

Trade and Industry, SADC countries have found themselves in no less than five negotiating configurations. Moreover, the way the negotiations unfolded in the course of 2007 created some very severe contradictions within SACU.

Part of the problem is that South Africa did not want to negotiate a trade in services agreement, as proposed by the EU, because South Africa has very few potential opportunities in services in the European market, whereas the Europeans have many in the South African market.

South Africa would be interested in a multilateral services agreement through the WTO, provided it can be sufficiently structured to be developmental in its focus, but has very little interest in a bilateral agreement with the EU in services. So South Africa was at this stage only interested in an agreement on cooperation around building capacity to negotiate service agreements. South Africa's also said that it would not want to negotiate binding commitments on the Singapore issues, which relate to investment agreements with rights of establishment, competition, intellectual property and government procurement. The EU wanted South Africa's competition authorities to intervene on behalf of European firms against domestic monopolies. Another issue relates to tariffs, because the EU uses public and private standards on things like food safety and chemicals regulations to keep out African products.

However, the EPA process has proceeded with many other problems. For example, there was a ban on export taxes, something which is quite important for South Africa's minerals beneficiation strategy. South Africa also felt that the institutional arrangements of the EPA would create powerful machinery that could trump decisions in either the SADC or SACU structures. And then South Africa faced a very important clause, something called a More Favoured Nation clause, which prescribed that if it gave any other country that had more than 1 per cent of world trade (that is, China, India and Brazil) better trading terms than it gives to the EU, then South Africa would have to extend the same terms to the EU.

That clause is in conflict with the enabling clause of the WTO agreement, which allows developing countries to reach more preferential arrangements among themselves. It would be a major barrier to trade diversification, moving away from just a relationship with one or a few groups of countries and a major barrier to developing South–South trade. So South Africa declined to sign. But some members of SACU have done so, which has created a major problem in SACU. For instance, Namibia was faced with a choice of either initialling an Interim EPA or facing 90 per cent duties on its beef.

The Interim EPAs included a commitment to negotiate a trade-in-services agreement, starting with one particular sector over the course of 2008 and then full liberalisation towards the EU of 'substantially all' services sectors within four years. They also included a commitment to start negotiations on the Singapore issues with an investment agreement.

The official SADC approach to the EU's EPA strategy was initially nuanced and premised upon various preconditions. The framework was sent to the EC in March 2006, and SADC member states wished to 'retain sovereignty over the regional integration agenda and timetable [and over] the time and policy options to define a regionally determined approach to harmonise their tariff structures'. The 'process of regional integration was paramount.'

According to Keet, SADC indicated that the 'new generation issues' should have no place in the EPA negotiations as they pose serious 'policy challenges' and could create 'imbalanced outcomes that may be prejudicial to national development objectives and to prospects for deeper integration in SADC'. Also, some very useful aspects of South Africa's Trade, Development and Cooperation Agreement (TDCA) with the EU were incorporated into the SADC framework for negotiating with the EU.

After a delay of a full year, the EC eventually responded in March 2007 to the SADC framework stating that there was no possibility of revising the TDCA in the way that the SADC paper suggested. They also demanded that Botswana, Lesotho, Namibia and Swaziland and the other LDCs in SADC must offer some levels of reciprocity to the EU in return for the 'duty free and quota free' access to the EU market. The 'reciprocity' to the EU from the SADC countries must also take the form of accepting the inclusion of 'new generation' issues in SADC–EU negotiations. Furthermore, the 'development cooperation' aid and assistance that SADC sought would be lost unless they signed an EPA, because the EDF (European Development Fund) is now earmarked for the implementation of EPAs.

Similar conditions applied to other trading blocks of the developing countries. Keet argues that opening up these regions to EU producers/exporters will enable them to compete with ACP producers/traders within their own national markets as well as in the markets of other countries in their regions. In this way, EPAs will undermine one of the main aims of regional integration, which is to create combined and enlarged markets to encourage local, national and regional producers and the expansion of intra-regional trade.

Also, by pushing these regions towards rapid trade liberalisation, the EPAs will also contradict the need for different rates of tariff reductions, arrived at through negotiated multilateral trade agreements between the members of such regions. Such variable tariff reductions are essential in order to give a measure of protection to weaker producers and traders within a region and to counter the advantages of the larger and/or more economically advanced of regional members, such as Kenya within the East African Community (EAC), or South Africa within SADC.

Despite these many problems, the EC has assured the ACP regions that they can rely on 'international expertise' – meaning

EU investment/production and planning/research services backed up by EU financial and technical 'development' aid. However, this will typically go mainly to European consultants and companies.

Keet argues that the situation in which the SADC group finds itself is somewhat similar to that of the Central African group of countries, which made a commitment to conclude EPAs with the EC by June 2008. The region is at a point where it has agreed to a negotiation 'road map' with the EC that will pave the way towards a comprehensive trade liberalisation deal. Divisions within the Central African group were sown when Cameroon unilaterally signed an interim agreement with the EC, which will see the country benefiting from a zero-rate tariff for exporting bananas into the EU. The EU will, however, benefit even more by having tariffs eliminated on over 80 per cent of its imported goods. It is understood among authorities in Central Africa that this will lead to massive revenue losses; to make up for these, Cameroon will have to put in place more effective fiscal policies in the domestic economy. This eventuality may harm the Central African region in another way, as the EU may well use Cameroon to import its goods into the region, which generally does not have capacity to effectively impose the rules on imports.

Due to concerns over the robust nature of the EC proposals and the disparate positions held by the various stakeholders, which threaten regional unity, it was resolved at the Second EU–Africa Summit that the AU Commission meet with its counterpart, the European Commission, in order to discuss the terms of reference for the full EPA negotiations before individual countries begin their own talks: 'The AU declaration on EPAs, issued at the AU Summit in Ethiopia, called for a review of the interim EPAs, in line with concerns raised at the EU–Africa Summit. The AU Assembly issued a further mandate to the AU Commission to "coordinate, monitor and harmonise efforts of AU Member States in the EPA negotiations with the European Union".'

The EPA process, rather than being something that will help advance development and regional integration, looks like becoming an obstacle that will have to be overcome in pursuit of these objectives.

The negotiations on EPAs have reached a turning point. Many of the protagonists are not content with the deal offered by the EU. Experts and analysts have warned that the current deals may threaten to undermine development. These matters require the urgent attention of Africa's parliamentarians, who are the custodians of the people's interests. It is hoped that the Pan-African Parliament can take this forward vigorously.

Sources

Chang, Ha-Joon (2002). Kicking away the ladder. London: Anthem Press.

Davies, Rob (2008). 'The Economic Partnership Agreements, now pending between South Africa and Europe', in *New Agenda: South African Journal of Social and Economic Policy*, Issue 30, Second quarter.

Department of Trade and Industry (DTI) (2008). 'SADC EPA–EC negotiations. Assessing the emerging outcome', 30 January 2008.

Dieter, Heribert (2006). 'Australia's trade agreement with the United States'. Paper for Global Governance Challenges, SWP Workshop, Berlin, 9–10 March 2006.

Keet, Dot (2007). 'Economic Partnership Agreements: Europe's latest economic policy offensive against Africa'. *New Agenda: South African Journal of Social and Economic Policy*, Issue 30, Second quarter; AIDC, 9 August 2007.

Khor, Martin (2008). 'Horizontal process postponed'. *Third World Economics*, 16 March: p. 2.

Parliament of South Africa, Research Unit (2008). Economic Partnership Agreements (EPA) Update, 25 February 2008.

Additional sources

AU Declaration on Economic Partnership Agreements DCC. X.CU394 (XII).

Central Africa EPAs and regional Integration, IPSNews.net, 18 February 2008. Available from http://www.tralac.org/scripts/content.php/id=7351.

Economic Partnership Agreements: What happens in 2008? Oversees Development Institute Briefing Paper no. 23, June 2007.

European Research Office, Main issues in Africa–EU EPA Negotiations, January 2007.

Le Roux, M. (2008). 'Local textile and clothing sector faces blow as BA shuns EU trade deal', in *Business Day*, 19 February 2008.

Le Roux, M. (2008). 'SA–EU trade row puts customs union at risk', in *Business Day*, 25 February 2008.

Lynn, J. 'Trade talks still struggle but farms get boost', Reuters.com.

Weidlich, B. (2008). 'Namibia: EPAs "might threaten regional integration"', in *The Namibian*, 15 February 2008. Available from http://www.tralac.org/scripts/content.php?id=7350; accessed 22 December 2010.

Index